SCHOLASTIC

T0326061

GCSE 9-1 CHEMISTRY AQA EXAM PRACTICE

Sarah Carter and Darren Grover

Author Sarah Carter and Darren Grover
Editorial team Haremi Ltd
Series designers emc design ltd
Typesetting Newgen KnowledgeWorks (P) Ltd, Chennai, India
Illustrations York Publishing Services and Newgen KnowledgeWorks (P) Ltd, Chennai, India
App development Hannah Barnett, Phil Crothers and Haremi Ltd

Designed using Adobe InDesign
Published by Scholastic Education, an imprint of Scholastic Ltd, Book End, Range Road, Witney, Oxfordshire, OX29 0YD
Registered office: Westfield Road, Southam, Warwickshire CV47 0RA
www.scholastic.co.uk

Printed by Bell & Bain Ltd, Glasgow
© 2017 Scholastic Ltd
1 2 3 4 5 6 7 8 9   7 8 9 0 1 2 3 4 5 6

British Library Cataloguing-in-Publication Data
A catalogue record for this book is available from the British Library.
ISBN 978-1407-17679-6

Notes from the publisher

Please use this product in conjunction with the official specification and sample assessment materials. Ask your teacher if you are unsure where to find them.

The marks and star ratings have been suggested by our subject experts, but they are to be used as a guide only.

Answer space has been provided, but you may need to use additional paper for your workings.

Contents

Topic 7 ORGANIC CHEMISTRY

Topic 8 CHEMICAL ANALYSIS

Topic 9 CHEMISTRY OF THE ATMOSPHERE

Topic 10 USING RESOURCES

PAPER 1

ANSWERS

How to use this book

This Exam Practice Book has been produced to help you revise for your 9–1 GCSE in AQA Chemistry. Written by experts and packed full of exam-style questions for each subtopic, along with full practice papers, it will get you exam ready!

The best way to retain information is to take an active approach to revision. Don't just read the information you need to remember – do something with it! Transforming information from one form into another and applying your knowledge will ensure that it really sinks in. Throughout this book you'll find lots of features that will make your revision practice an active, successful process.

EXAM-STYLE QUESTIONS
Exam-style questions for each subtopic ramped in difficulty.

H Higher Tier-only content is highlighted helping you to target your revision

DOIT!
Tasks that support your understanding and analysis of a question.

WORKIT!
Worked examples with model solutions to help you see how to answer a tricky question.

Callouts Step-by-step guidance to build understanding.

NAILIT!
Tips to help you perform in the exam.

STRETCHIT!
Questions or concepts that stretch you further and challenge you with the most difficult content.

★ STAR RATING ★
A quick visual guide to indicate the difficulty of the question, with 1 star representing the least demanding and 5 stars signposting the most challenging questions.

MARKS (5 marks)
Each question has the number of marks available to help you target your response.

▌ PRACTICE PAPERS
Full mock-exam papers to enable you to have a go at a complete paper before you sit the real thing! Find Paper 2 online at www.scholastic.co.uk/gcse

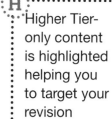

Use the AQA Chemistry Revision Guide alongside the Exam Practice Book for a complete revision and practice solution. Written by a subject expert to match the new specification, the Revision Guide uses an active approach to revise all the content you need to know!

HOW TO REVISE!

PLAN YOUR REVISION

Get ahead by planning your revision!

Work out the **time** you have available for revising.

Think about when you work at your best. Are you a morning or an evening person?

Allocate **MORE TIME** for the topics you struggle with.

Revision works best in **SMALL BURSTS**, so keep sessions **SHORT AND SWEET**!

Remember to allow time to **PRACTISE** applying what you have revised.

Use your **revision app** to put together a revision timetable.

LOOK AFTER YOURSELF

Help your brain by looking after your whole body!

Take regular **breaks** from revising – your brain needs time to digest information in order to retain it.

HOTEL

Keep **hydrated** by drinking plenty of water – dehydration stops your brain from working at its full capacity.

Regular **exercise** helps stimulate the brain and will help you relax.

Get plenty of **sleep**, especially the night before an exam.

EAT WELL and limit unhealthy snacks – your brain needs fuel for memory and concentration.

Find methods of **relaxation** that work for you throughout the revision period.

BE PREPARED!

Limit potential stress on the day of an exam by getting everything you need ready the night before.

30

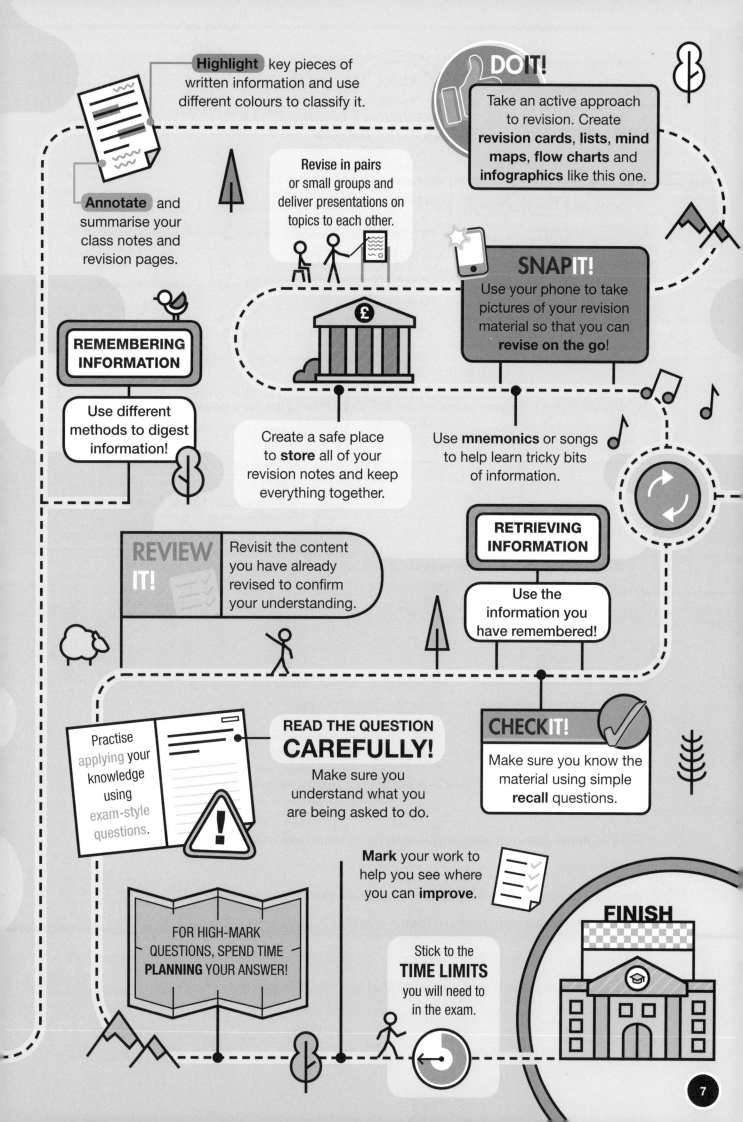

Highlight key pieces of written information and use different colours to classify it.

DO IT!
Take an active approach to revision. Create **revision cards**, **lists**, **mind maps**, **flow charts** and **infographics** like this one.

Annotate and summarise your class notes and revision pages.

Revise in pairs or small groups and deliver presentations on topics to each other.

SNAP IT!
Use your phone to take pictures of your revision material so that you can **revise on the go!**

REMEMBERING INFORMATION

Use different methods to digest information!

Create a safe place to **store** all of your revision notes and keep everything together.

Use **mnemonics** or songs to help learn tricky bits of information.

REVIEW IT! Revisit the content you have already revised to confirm your understanding.

RETRIEVING INFORMATION

Use the information you have remembered!

Practise applying your knowledge using exam-style questions.

READ THE QUESTION CAREFULLY!
Make sure you understand what you are being asked to do.

CHECK IT!
Make sure you know the material using simple **recall** questions.

Mark your work to help you see where you can **improve**.

FOR HIGH-MARK QUESTIONS, SPEND TIME **PLANNING** YOUR ANSWER!

Stick to the **TIME LIMITS** you will need to in the exam.

FINISH

Atomic structure and the periodic table

Atoms, elements and compounds

(1) **This question is about atoms, elements and compounds.**

a **Draw one line from each word to its correct description.** (4 marks, ★★)

Atom	A substance that contains two or more elements chemically combined.
Element	A substance that contains two or more elements not chemically combined.
Compound	A substance made of only one type of atom.
Mixture	The smallest part of an element that can exist.

b **Which of the following substances are elements? Tick two boxes.** (2 marks, ★★)

Br_2	
Na_2CO_3	
Ar	
H_2O	

DO IT!

Look through your Revision Guide for different formulae, and then work out the numbers of each type of element present. This will also help to familiarise you with the different substances you need to know.

c **Which of the following represents a compound? Tick one box.** (1 mark, ★★)

A

B

C

D

A	
B	
C	
D	

d **How many atoms are there in a particle of magnesium nitrate, $Mg(NO_3)_2$?** (1 mark, ★★★)

....

e **How many different elements are there in a particle of sulfuric acid, H_2SO_4?** (1 mark, ★★★)

....

(2) **Use your periodic table to help you to answer the following questions.**

a **Name two elements that are found in group 7.** (2 marks, ★)

....

b **Give the symbols of two elements that are found in group 1.** (2 marks, ★) ....

Mixtures and compounds

(1) **Place each substance under the correct heading in the table below.** (3 marks, ★)

| air | salty water | oxygen |
| hydrogen | water | sodium hydroxide |

Element	Compound	Mixture

(2) **A student prepares a soluble salt by reacting copper(II) oxide with hydrochloric acid. He ends up with a solution of copper(II) chloride. Describe how solid copper(II) chloride could be obtained from this mixture.** (2 marks, ★★)

....

....

(3) **A mixture of salt and water can be separated by simple distillation. Ethanol boils at 78°C and water boils at 100°C.**

a **Name the piece of apparatus labelled A.**
(1 mark, ★)

....

b **Explain how pure water is obtained during this process.** (3 marks, ★★★)

....

....

....

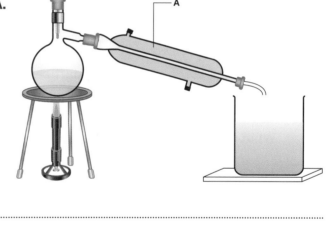

....

....

....

(4) **Rock salt is a naturally-occurring mineral that consists of a mixture of sodium chloride and sand. Sodium chloride is soluble in water and sand is insoluble in water. Describe how both the sodium chloride and sand could be separately extracted from the rock salt.**
(4 marks, ★★★)

....

....

....

....

....

....

Scientific models of the atom

1. **How did scientists describe the structure of the atom before electrons were discovered?**
(2 marks, ★★)

....

....

2. **The plum pudding model was then suggested after the discovery of the electron. The image to the right shows a diagram of this model. Describe what the plum pudding model shows.**
(2 marks, ★★)

....

....

....

3. **Further experiments by Rutherford tested the plum pudding model by firing alpha particles at gold foil. Instead of them all passing through the foil, some of them were deflected.**

   a **What is the charge on an alpha particle?** (1 mark, ★)

   ....

   b **Why did most of them pass through the gold foil?** (1 mark, ★★)

   ....

   c **Why were some of the alpha particles deflected?** (1 mark, ★★)

   ....

   d **What was the overall conclusion from this experiment?** (2 marks, ★★★)

   ....

   ....

   e **Which sub-atomic particle did Chadwick prove existed in the nucleus?** (1 mark, ★★)

   ....

NAILIT!

The main fact that you need to know about the development of the atomic model is how Rutherford's scattering experiment changed scientists' ideas about the plum pudding model.

Atomic structure, isotopes and relative atomic mass

(1) **Complete the table of the relative charges and masses of the sub-atomic particles.**
(3 marks, ★★)

Sub-atomic particle	Relative charge	Relative mass
	+1	
		Very small
Neutron		

NAILIT!

Learn the names of the sub-atomic particles, along with their relative masses and charges; this is often assessed in exam questions.

(2) **Explain why the overall charge of a magnesium atom is neutral.** (2 marks, ★★)

....

....

(3) **Element Z has a mass number of 184 and an atomic number of 74.**

a **Calculate the number of protons, electrons and neutrons in an atom of Z.** (2 marks, ★★)

....

....

b **Use the periodic table to identify the name of element Z.** (1 mark, ★★)

....

DOIT!

You could be asked questions about any element in the periodic table. Pick random elements and calculate the number of protons, electrons and neutrons in each. This will also help to familiarise you with the periodic table!

(4) **Use the words in the box below to complete the following passage about isotopes. You will not need to use all of the words, and some words may be used more than once.**

Isotopes of an element have the same .... number but a different .... number.

This means that atoms of the same element have the same number of .... but different

numbers of .... Two isotopes of carbon are C-12 and C-13. Both of these isotopes have

.... protons; however, C-12 has .... neutrons and C-13 has .... neutrons. (3 marks, ★★)

12	atomic	7	neutrons	electrons	6	mass	13	protons

(5) **There are two naturally-occurring isotopes of bromine, Br-79 and Br-81.**

Describe the similarities and differences between these two isotopes, referring to the number of sub-atomic particles in your answer. (3 marks, ★★★★)

....

....

....

(6) **The relative atomic mass of chlorine is 35.5. Chlorine exists as two isotopes, one of which is Cl-35. This makes up 75% of naturally occurring chlorine. Use this information to calculate the mass number of the other isotope of chlorine.** (3 marks, ★★★★★)

....

....

The development of the periodic table and the noble gases

1. **Use your periodic table to answer the following questions.** (4 marks, ★★)

    a Carbon is in group .... of the periodic table.

    b Potassium is in period .... of the periodic table.

    c Why are phosphorous and nitrogen placed in the same group?

    ....

    d Why are sulfur and silicon placed in the same period?

    ....

DO IT!

Early versions of the periodic table show the elements that had been discovered placed in order of increasing atomic weight. Why?

2. **Mendeleev decided to arrange the elements according to their properties. The table below shows an early version of his periodic table.**

Row	Group I	Group II	Group III	Group IV	Group V	Group VI	Group VII	Group VIII
1	H							
2	Li	Be	B	C	N	O	F	
3	Na	Mg	Al	Si	P	S	Cl	
4	K	Ca		Ti	V	Cr	Mn	Fe, Co, Ni, Cu

    a What is the correct name for the horizontal rows in the periodic table? (1 mark, ★)

    ....

    b Why did Mendeleev leave gaps? (1 mark, ★★)

    ....

    c How are the elements arranged in the modern version of the periodic table? (1 mark, ★★)

    ....

    d Suggest why it took a long time for the noble gases to be discovered. (1 mark, ★★)

    ....

3. **The noble gases are found in group 0 of the periodic table, their boiling points are shown in the table below.**

    a What is the trend in boiling points?
    (1 mark, ★★)

    ....

    b Predict the boiling point of krypton.
    (1 mark, ★★)

    ....

Noble gas	Boiling point/°C
He	−269
Ne	−246
Ar	−186
Kr	
Xe	−108
Rn	−62

Electronic structure

1 The diagram represents an element from the periodic table.

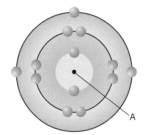

a What is the name of the part labelled A? (1 mark, ★★)

....

b What are the names of the sub-atomic particles found in A? (2 marks, ★★)

....

....

The mass number of this element is 27.

c Name the element represented by this diagram. (1 mark, ★★)

....

d How many neutrons does this element have? (1 mark, ★★)

....

2 The electronic structures of six elements, A, B, C, D, E and F, are shown below.

2, 8, 8, 1

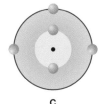

2, 8

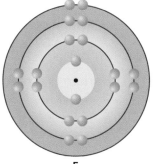

Use the correct letter or letters to answer each question.

a Which atom represents an element in group 3? (1 mark, ★)

b Which element has the symbol O? (1 mark, ★★)

c Which **two** elements are in the same group? (2 marks, ★★)

d Which **two** elements are in period 4? (2 marks, ★★)

e Which element is a noble gas? (1 mark, ★★)

f Which element forms a 2⁻ ion? (1 mark, ★★★)

Metals and non-metals

(1) **Match up these words with their correct meanings.** (3 marks, ★)

Malleable	Makes a ringing sound when hit
Ductile	Can be hammered into shape
Sonorous	Can be drawn into wires

(2) **Some elements in the periodic table are highlighted below.**

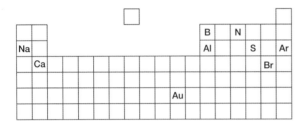

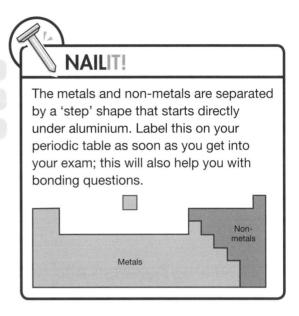

NAILIT!

The metals and non-metals are separated by a 'step' shape that starts directly under aluminium. Label this on your periodic table as soon as you get into your exam; this will also help you with bonding questions.

Choose the correct element to answer each question. (1 mark each)

a Which element is in group 1? (★) ....

b Which element is used in jewellery? (★) ....

c Which element has a mass number of 32? (★★) ....

d Which element is a noble gas? ....

e Which element is a non-metal in group 3? (★★★) ....

f Which element is a non-metal in period 4? (★★★) ....

g Which element forms a 2+ ion? (★★★) ....

h Which element forms a 3– ion? (★★★★) ....

(3) **Barium is a reactive element found in group 2 of the periodic table.**

a **Is barium a metal or a non-metal?** (1 mark, ★)

....

b **How many electrons does barium have in its outer shell?** (1 mark, ★)

....

c **Which two properties would you expect barium to have? Circle the correct answer.** (2 marks, ★★)

| low melting point   good electrical conductor   brittle   shiny |

Group 1 – the alkali metals

(1) **Explain, using electron configuration, why all the group 1 metals have similar chemical properties.** (1 mark, ★★)

....

(2) **Circle which group 1 metal is represented by the symbol K.** (1 mark, ★)

Lithium	Sodium	Potassium	Krypton

(3) **Circle which is the most reactive group 1 metal.** (1 mark, ★)

Sodium	Caesium	Lithium	Francium

(4) **The diagram shows the electronic structure of a group 1 metal.** (1 mark, ★★★)

What is the symbol for this metal?

N	K	Na	Li

Symbol: ....

(5) **A student watches the reaction of lithium with water.**

State three observations the student would see during the reaction. (3 marks, ★★★)

....

....

....

(6) **Potassium reacts with water in a similar way to lithium.**

State two observations that would be different. (2 marks, ★★★)

....

....

Group 7 – the halogens

① **Circle the chemical symbol for fluorine.** (1 mark, ★)

| Fl | Fr | F | Fe |

② **Circle the most reactive halogen.** (1 mark, ★)

| Bromine | Iodine | Chlorine | Fluorine |

③ **Circle the correct formula for a molecule of bromine.** (1 mark, ★★★)

| Be | Br | B_2 | Br_2 |

④ **Circle which halogen has the electronic configuration 2,8,7.** (1 mark, ★★★)

| Chlorine | Bromine | Fluorine | Iodine |

DO IT!

When the halogens react, they change the ending of their name from **ine** to **ide**. Practise writing simple word equations to get used to this!

e.g. sodium + chlorine → sodium chloride

NAIL IT!

The halogens can react with other non-metals to form **covalent** substances. They can also react with metals to form **ionic** substances.

⑤ **A student watches the reaction between lithium and chlorine, and lithium and iodine.**

a **Which would be the most vigorous reaction? Explain why.** (1 mark, ★★)

b **Write a word equation for the reaction between lithium and chlorine.** (1 mark, ★★)

c **Write a balanced symbol equation for the reaction between lithium and iodine.** (2 marks, ★★★★)

⑥ **The reactivity of chlorine, bromine and iodine can be shown by carrying out reactions between these halogens and solutions of their salts.**

	Chlorine	Bromine	Iodine
Potassium chloride	x	No reaction	
Potassium bromide	Orange solution formed	x	No reaction
Potassium iodide			x

a **Complete the table, stating any colour changes that would take place.** (3 marks, ★★)

b **Write a word equation for the reaction between chlorine and potassium bromide.** (1 mark, ★★)

c **On a separate piece of paper suggest an experiment that you could carry out to prove that iodine is more reactive than astatine. State what you would observe and write down a chemical equation and an ionic equation for this reaction.** (4 marks, ★★★★★)

The transition metals

1 Which of the following metals are transition metals? Circle **three** elements. (3 marks, ★★)

| silver   tin   mercury   magnesium   tungsten |

DOIT!

You need to be able to compare the properties of the transition metals with those of group 1. Construct a table like this to show the similarities and differences.

Property	Group 1 metal	Transition metals
Melting and boiling points		
Electrical conductivity		
Reactivity		
Density		

2 Palladium, Pd, is a transition metal which is used in jewellery and also in catalytic converters in cars.

a Suggest a property of palladium that makes it suitable for use in jewellery. (1 mark, ★)

....

b Predict **three** properties of palladium that would be different from sodium. (3 marks, ★★)

....

....

....

3 A student watches the reaction between sodium and chlorine. The reaction is vigorous and the sodium burns brightly with a yellow flame, producing a solid product.

NAILIT!

Make sure you know the differences between the properties of the metals and their compounds. For example, copper metal is orange/bronze-coloured, but copper compounds are usually blue or green.

a **Name the solid formed.** (1 mark, ★)

....

b **State the colour of the solid formed.** (1 mark, ★★)

....

c **Write a balanced symbol equation for this reaction.** (2 marks, ★★★★)

....

....

4 Iron also reacts with chlorine. In this reaction there are two possible products, iron(II) chloride and iron(III) chloride.

Would the reaction of iron with chlorine be more or less vigorous than the reaction of sodium with chlorine? Explain your answer. (1 mark, ★★)

....

Bonding and structure

① **Complete the boxes below by choosing the correct words which represent these changes of state.** (4 marks, ★)

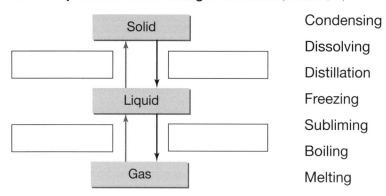

Condensing

Dissolving

Distillation

Freezing

Subliming

Boiling

Melting

> **NAILIT!**
>
> The **boiling point** is the temperature at which a liquid boils and turns into a gas, *or* condenses from a gas to a liquid.
>
> The **melting point** is the temperature at which a solid melts, *or* when a liquid freezes and turns into a solid.

② **Water freezes at 0°C and turns into ice. It boils at 100°C and turns into water vapour.** (2 marks, ★★)

a **What is the melting point of water?** ....

b **At what temperature will water vapour condense back into a liquid?** ....

③ **Mercury, Hg, melts at –39°C and boils at 357°C. Use this information to predict the state of mercury at the following temperatures.** (3 marks, ★★★)

a **500°C** .... b **–40°C** ....

c **Room temperature, 25°C** ....

④ **Air consists of a mixture of several different gases, some of which are shown in the table below.**

Gas	Boiling point/°C
Nitrogen	–196
Oxygen	–183
Argon	–186

The gases can be separated by fractional distillation; this involves cooling the air down and removing each gas as it condenses. (4 marks, ★★★)

a **Which gas has the highest boiling point?** ....

b **Which gas has the lowest boiling point?** ....

c **Which gas would condense first when air is cooled?** ....

d **Which gas has the strongest forces between its particles?** ....

Ions and ionic bonding

(1) **Complete the following passage using the words below. Some words may be used more than once.**

Magnesium is a metal which is found in group .... of the periodic table. This means it has .... electrons in its outer shell. When it reacts, it loses .... electrons and forms an ion with a .... charge. Fluorine is a non-metal which is found in group .... of the periodic table. When it reacts, it .... 1 electron to form an ion with a .... charge. When magnesium reacts with fluorine, it forms magnesium fluoride which has the formula .... (8 marks, ★★)

MgF	1	2	3	gains	Mg$_2$F	6	
7	loses	MgF$_2$	1⁻	2⁻	1⁺	2⁺	

MgF   1   2   3   gains   Mg$_2$F   6
7   loses   MgF$_2$ 1⁻   2⁻   1⁺   2⁺

> **NAILIT!**
>
> Use the periodic table when you tackle any questions about bonding. First of all, make sure you know where the metals and non-metals are found; this will help you to determine the *type* of bonding. Secondly, remember that the group number tells you *how many electrons* are found in the outer shell.

(2) **Match the compound to its correct formula.** (4 marks, ★★)

Potassium chloride

Magnesium oxide

Magnesium chloride

Aluminium fluoride

K$_2$Cl

MgO$_2$

MgCl$_2$

Al$_3$F

KCl

AlF$_3$

MgO

KCl$_2$

DO IT!

> Practise writing out formulae by using the group numbers of the elements to find out the charge on the ions formed. Remember, *metals* form *positive ions* and *non-metals* form *negative ions*. Then, work out the number of each ion needed to make the charges add up to zero.
>
> For example, potassium is in group 1 so forms an ion with a 1⁺ charge, K⁺.
>
> Oxygen is in group 6 so forms an ion with a 2⁻ charge, O^{2-}.
>
> K⁺   O^{2-}
>
> There are 2 negative charges, but only 1 positive charge. Therefore, 2 positive charges are needed to cancel out the 2 negative charges which means we need to multiply the K⁺ by 2.
>
> 2 × K⁺   O^{2-}
>
> Overall, the formula is K$_2$O.

(3) **Draw dot and cross diagrams (outer electrons only) to show the formation of the ionic compounds below. For each diagram, work out the formula of the compound formed.**

a Lithium chloride (3 marks, ★★)

b Barium bromide (3 marks, ★★★)

The structure and properties of ionic compounds

① **Tick three boxes that describe the correct properties of ionic compounds.** (3 marks, ★★)

High melting points	
Made of molecules	
Conduct electricity when solid	
Conduct electricity when molten or in solution	
Made of non-metals bonded together	
Made of ions	

② **From the diagrams below, give one substance A, B or C that:**

a **represents sodium chloride, NaCl.** (★) ....

b **represents magnesium chloride, MgCl$_2$.** (★★) ....

c **represents sodium oxide.** (★★★) ....

(3 marks)

A   B   C

> **NAILIT!**
>
> Remember, ionic compounds only conduct electricity when molten or dissolved in water, because the ions are free to move, not the electrons! Make sure you use the correct charge carrier!

③ **Complete the following passage about the structure of ionic compounds, choosing the correct words from the box below.** (3 marks, ★★)

Ionic bonds are formed when .... react with .... Atoms either lose or gain

.... to become positive or negative particles called ions. The ions are held together in a

giant ionic .... by strong .... forces of attraction acting in all ....

magnetic	protons	metals	areas	electrostatic	molecules
directions	neutrons	lattice	non-metals	electrons	

④ **Potassium iodide is a substance that is often added to table salt in countries where people have little iodine in their diets. A deficiency of iodine can cause many long-term health problems but is also easily preventable. Use your ideas about structure and bonding to make predictions about the properties of potassium iodide.** (6 marks, ★★★★)

....

....

....

....

....

....

Covalent bonds and simple molecules

(1) **Which of the following substances are covalent? Tick each correct box.** (2 marks, ★★)

| NaCl |
| CaO |
| NH_3 |
| Potassium nitrate |
| Water |

(2) **The compounds drawn below all have covalent bonds.**

   a **Complete the dot and cross diagrams below to show the covalent bonding in each molecule.** (6 marks, ★★)

   b **Write out the formula of each substance.** (2 marks, ★★)

Hydrogen

Formula:

Methane

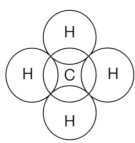

Formula:

(3) a **Draw a dot and cross diagram to show the bonding in a molecule of nitrogen, N_2.**
    (2 marks, ★★★★)

   b **What type of covalent bond does it have?** (1 mark, ★★★★) ....

(4) a **Ethene is a hydrocarbon with the formula C_2H_4. Draw a dot and cross diagram to show its bonding.** (2 marks, ★★★★★)

   b **What type of covalent bonds does it have?** (2 marks, ★★★★) ....

Diamond, graphite and graphene

(1) **Figure 1 shows three giant covalent substances. Choose the correct letter to answer each question.** (2 marks, ★★)

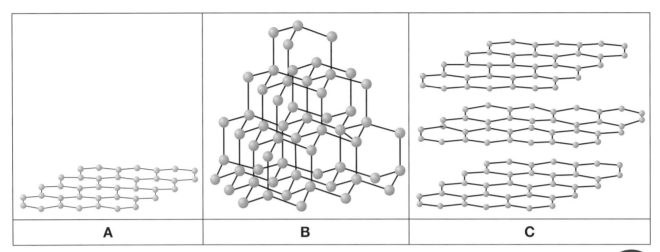

| A | B | C |

Figure 1

   a Which substance is graphene? ....

   b Which substance has weak intermolecular forces? ....

(2) **This question is about the properties of diamond and graphite.**

   a Use your knowledge about their structure and bonding to explain why diamond and graphite both have high melting points. (2 marks, ★★★)

   ....

   ....

   b **Explain why diamond is hard.** (2 marks, ★★★)

   ....

   ....

   c Although graphite is a non-metal, like metals it conducts electricity. Explain what feature both graphite and metals have that enable them to conduct electricity.
      (1 mark, ★★★)

   ....

(3) **Silicon dioxide, SiO_2, is the main component of sand. It has a giant covalent structure, shown below.**

   a **SiO_2 does *not* conduct electricity. Suggest why.**
      (1 mark, ★★★)

   ....

   b **Predict two further properties of SiO_2.** (2 marks, ★★★)

   ....

Fullerenes and polymers

① The diagram below shows three different substances made from carbon. Choose the correct letter to answer each question. (4 marks, ★★)

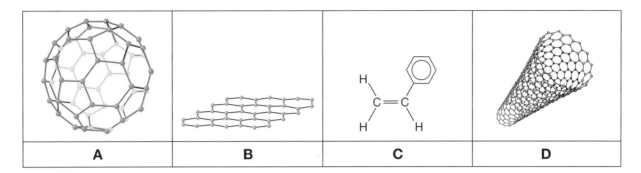

A	B	C	D

a Which substance has a very high length to diameter ratio? ....

b Which substance could be used to make a polymer? ....

c Which substance is buckminster fullerene? ....

d Which substance is made from a single layer of graphite? ....

② The structures of fullerenes and nanotubes are unique, which gives them many uses. Explain how their structure makes them suitable for the following:

a Fullerenes can be used to deliver drugs to targeted areas inside the body. (1 mark, ★★★)

....

b Nanotubes make excellent catalysts. (1 mark, ★★★)

....

③ Polyethene is a polymer made from many ethene molecules joined together in a long chain.

a Which type of bonds are found in polymers? (1 mark, ★)

....

The table below shows some of the properties of ethene and polyethene.

	Ethene	Polyethene
Melting point/°C	−169	Approx. 120
Size of molecules	Small	Large
State at room temperature	Gas	Solid

b Use this information to explain why ethene is a gas at room temperature yet polyethene is a solid. (3 marks, ★★★)

....

....

....

Giant metallic structures and alloys

DO IT!

The properties of metals depend on their structure and bonding. Practise drawing *labelled* diagrams to represent metallic bonding. This will help you to gain marks in exam questions.

NAILIT!

The difference in the properties between pure metals and alloys is all down to the *sizes* of the atoms and the *distortion* of the regular layers of atoms.

(1) **Use the words in the box below to complete the following passage about metals. You will not need to use all of the words.** (4 marks, ★★)

Metals are .... structures.

The atoms are arranged in ....

The outer shell electrons become detached from the rest of the atom and are said to be .... This means they are free to move throughout the whole metal.

Metallic bonding is strong because of the .... attraction between the positive metal ions and the electrons.

| layers | magnetic | giant | electrostatic | small | delocalised |

(2) **Explain, with the aid of a labelled diagram, why metals are good electrical conductors.** (4 marks,****)

....

....

....

....

(3) **Iron is the fourth most abundant element found in the Earth's crust, and has many different uses.**

a **The melting point of pure iron is 1538°C. Explain this in terms of metallic bonding.** (2 marks,**)

....

....

Pure iron is relatively soft, so is often mixed with other elements to form alloys. Steel is made when small amounts of carbon are added to iron.

b **Explain why steel is harder than pure iron.** (2 marks,***)

....

....

Nanoparticles

(1) Which is the correct size range of a nanoparticle?
Tick one box. (1 mark, ★)

1–1000 nm	
1–100 mm	
1–100 nm	
1–1000 mm	

NAILIT!

Surface area of a cube = side^2 × volume of a cube = side^3

Surface area to volume ratio = surface area/volume

WORKIT!

Convert 15 nanometres to metres and express your answer in standard form. (1 mark, ★★★)

You must be able to express your answers in standard form. We are dealing with very small numbers here so we will concentrate on these.

- First, convert 15 nanometres to metres. 1 nanometre is equivalent to 0.000000001, or $1 × 10^{-9}$ metres. Therefore, 15 nanometres is 0.000000015 metres.
- Look for the first number which is not 0 after the decimal point. In this case it's number 1.
- Count how many places it is after the decimal point – it's 8 places after. This means that your answer must have 10^{-8} in it.

0	.	0	0	0	0	0	0	0	1	5
		1	2	3	4	5	6	7	8	9

- Finally, look at the numbers which aren't 0. Put a decimal point after the first number which gives us 1.5.
  Put everything together to get the final answer of $1.5 × 10^{-8}$ m.

(2) Convert the following measurements to metres, expressing your answer in standard form.
(4 marks, ★★★)

a **86 nm** ....

c **158.6 nm** ....

b **14.6 nm** ....

d **8.2 nm** ....

e **Which of the above measurements does not correspond to a nanoparticle? Explain your answer.** (2 marks, ★★)

....

....

(3) A cube with sides of 50 nm has a surface area to volume ratio of 0.12.

a **Calculate the surface area to volume ratio of a cube with sides of 5 nm.** (3 marks, ★★★)

....

....

....

b **What is the relationship between the length of the side of the cube and the surface area to volume ratio?** (2 marks, ★★★★)

....

....

Quantitative chemistry

Conservation of mass and balancing equations

(1) **Magnesium burns in oxygen to produce magnesium oxide.**

a **Write a word equation for this reaction.** (2 marks, ★)

.... → ....

b **Identify the reactants and products in this reaction.** (2 marks, ★)

Reactants	Products

The reaction can also be written in a balanced equation as:

$2Mg + O_2 \rightarrow 2MgO$

c **If 12g of magnesium reacts with 8g of oxygen, what is the mass of MgO product?** (2 marks, ★)

....

NAILIT!

Don't forget that in all chemical reactions, the mass before and after the reaction is the same!

Think of it as like making a cake – the amount of flour, sugar, butter and eggs doesn't change after you bake them – they just react and turn into something new!

WORKIT!

When sodium reacts with water it produces sodium hydroxide and hydrogen gas. Balance the equation.

Step 1 Write a word equation for the reaction and identify the reactants and products:

Reactants			Products	
sodium	+	water	→ sodium hydroxide	+ hydrogen

Step 2 Write a symbol equation for the reaction:

Na + H_2O → $NaOH$ + H_2

Step 3 Count the number of atoms before and after the reaction:

$Na = 1$ → $Na = 1$

$O = 1$ $O = 1$

$H = 2$ $H = 3$

> We can see here that we end up with more hydrogen atoms than we started with – that's impossible!

Continued

WORKIT!

Step 4 Balance the equation by writing the number in front of the reactants or products, keeping count of the atoms as you go:

$$\underline{2}Na \quad + \quad \underline{2}H_2O \quad \rightarrow \quad \underline{2}NaOH \quad + \quad H_2$$

$$Na = 2 \qquad\qquad\qquad \rightarrow \quad Na = \underline{2}$$

$$O = 2 \qquad\qquad\qquad\qquad O = \underline{2}$$

$$H = 4 \qquad\qquad\qquad\qquad H = \underline{4}$$

Step 5 Write the balanced equation:

$$2Na \quad + \quad 2H_2O \quad \rightarrow \quad 2NaOH \quad + \quad H_2$$

Balancing and interpreting equations are really important skills that will be useful elsewhere in the exam, so spend some extra time making sure you're happy with them before moving on.

②　**The production of ammonia by reacting nitrogen and hydrogen is shown in the unbalanced equation below:** (4 marks, ★★★)

$N_2(g) + H_2(g) \rightarrow NH_3(g)$

a **Write a word equation for the reaction.**

....

b **Identify the number of atoms before and after the reaction in the unbalanced equation.**

	Reactants	Products
N		
H		

c **Write a balanced equation for this reaction.**

....

③　**Write a balanced equation for the reaction of iron oxide (Fe_2O_3) with carbon monoxide to produce iron and carbon dioxide.** (2 marks, ★★★★)

....

NAILIT!

Double check that you've balanced the equation correctly – count the number of atoms again! Remember, the number of atoms in the reactants and the products should be the same – if they aren't, it isn't balanced!

Relative formula masses

(1) **Match the following terms to their definition.** (2 marks, ★★)

The relative atomic mass (symbol = A_r)	of a compound by adding up all the relative atomic masses of all the atoms present in the formula of the compound.
You calculate the relative formula mass (symbol = M_r)	of an element is the weighted average mass of its naturally occurring isotopes.
The elements hydrogen, oxygen, nitrogen, chlorine, bromine, iodine and fluorine exist as diatomic molecules	means that in a chemical reaction the sum of the relative formula masses of the reactants is equal to the sum of the relative formula masses of the products.
The law of mass conservation	in equations their relative formula masses are twice their relative atomic masses.

(2) **Find the A_r for the following elements.** (3 marks, ★★)

Carbon	Oxygen	Chlorine	Iron
12			

(3) **A neutralisation reaction of sodium hydroxide and sulfuric acid is shown in the balanced equation:**

$2NaOH + H_2SO_4 \rightarrow Na_2SO_4 + 2H_2O$

a **Find the M_r for each of the reactants and products.** (4 marks, ★★)

NaOH	H_2SO_4	Na_2SO_4	H_2O

b **Calculate how much water is formed when 10 g of sulfuric acid reacts with excess sodium hydroxide.** (2 marks, ★★★★)

....

....

c **Calculate how much sodium hydroxide is needed to make 5 g of sodium sulfate.** (2 marks, ★★★★)

....

....

d **Suggest one reason why it is important that a company that produces sodium sulfate should know the mass of reactants.** (1 mark, ★★★★)

....

NAILIT!

- Remember that some elements are diatomic. HONClBrIF is one way to help you remember them!

- You will be given a periodic table in the exam – make sure you know which numbers refer to the relative atomic mass!

The mole and reactive masses

H(1) **Calculate the number of moles for the following.** (4 marks, ★★)

a 2.3g of sodium ....

b 1.6g of CH_4 ....

c 0.2g of SO_2 ....

d 2.2g of CO_2 ....

H(2) **Calculate the mass of the following.** (4 marks, ★★)

a 1.0mol HCl ....

b 1.5mol NaOH ....

c 0.3mol Na_2CO_3 ....

d 0.5mol $Al_2(SO_4)_3$ ....

H(3) **The labels on the containers of chemical substances in a laboratory have worn away and some of the information is missing. The information still visible has been recorded in the table below.**

Substance	A_r or M_r	Mass/g	Moles	Comments
Sodium	23.0	2.30	0.1	soft metal
		0.32	0.01	gas
CH_4		1.60		gas

a **Use the information available to complete the table.** (4 marks, ★★★)

   Another bottle contains hydrochloric acid (HCl) diluted in water. The label reads '50g HCl'.

b **Calculate the number of moles of HCl in the solution.** (2 marks, ★★★)

   ....

H(4) **Iron is an essential part of the human diet. Iron(II) sulfate is often added to breakfast cereals to supplement the iron from other sources in a person's diet. The formula for iron(II) sulfate is $FeSO_4$. Assume 1 mole of iron(II) sulfate produces 1 mole of iron.**

a **Calculate the M_r of $FeSO_4$.** (1 mark, ★★)

   ....

b **Calculate the mass of 0.25 moles of $FeSO_4$.** (1 mark, ★★★)

   ....

c **Calculate the mass of $FeSO_4$ needed to provide 7g of iron.** (2 marks, ★★★★)

   ....

d **Calculate the number of atoms of iron in 7g.** (2 marks, ★★★★)

   ....

H **(5)** Calcium carbonate undergoes thermal decomposition to produce calcium oxide and carbon dioxide as shown in the equation below:

$$CaCO_3(s) \rightarrow CaO(s) + CO_2(g)$$

a Calculate the mass of calcium oxide produced if 25 g of calcium carbonate decomposes. (2 marks, ★★★)

....

....

Carbon sequestration, storing carbon dioxide from the atmosphere in other forms, has been suggested as a way to reduce climate change caused by increased carbon dioxide in the atmosphere. Experiments have been conducted to find out whether calcium carbonate can be used in this way by reversing the thermal decomposition equation given above.

b Calculate the mass of calcium carbonate that would be produced by sequestering 500 kg of carbon dioxide. (2 marks, ★★★)

....

....

H **(6)** A pharmaceutical company produces tablets of the medicine paracetamol ($C_8H_9NO_2$), which contain 0.5 g of paracetamol.

a Calculate the number of moles of paracetamol in each tablet. (2 marks, ★★★)

....

....

b The same company produces the medicine aspirin by the following reaction:

$$C_7H_5O_3 + C_4H_6O_3 \rightarrow C_9H_8O_4 + CH_3COOH$$

salicylic acid + ethanoic anhydride → aspirin + ethanoic acid

(M_r = 138)   (M_r = 180)

Calculate the number of moles of aspirin produced if 4 g of salicylic acid is used. (2 marks, ★★★★)

....

....

c Calculate the number of molecules of salicylic acid that produce 0.5 g of aspirin. (2 marks, ★★★★)

....

....

....

MATHS SKILLS

Use the formulae for your calculations:

$n = m/M_r$, $m = n \times M_r$; no. of particles = $n \times N_A$

Don't forget to put the units in your answer and use standard form (e.g. 6.5×10^{-5} instead of 0.000065) when appropriate.

Limiting reactants

NAILIT!

A reaction stops when all the particles of one of the reactants are used up. In a reaction involving two reactants:

- the limiting reactant is the one that is all used up at the end of the reaction
- the reactant in excess is still there at the end of the reaction (although in a smaller amount than at the start).

H ① After a reaction of magnesium and hydrochloric acid, there is magnesium left behind.

a Which is the limiting reactant? (1 mark, ★) ....

b Which reactant was in excess? (1 mark, ★) ....

WORKIT!

In an experiment, 3.2 g of NH_3 reacts with 3.5 g of O_2. Find the limiting reactant.

$$NH_3 \quad + \quad O_2 \quad \rightarrow \quad NO \quad + \quad H_2O$$

Step 1 Balance the equation

$$4NH_3 \quad + \quad 5O_2 \quad \rightarrow \quad 4NO \quad + \quad 6H_2O$$

Step 2 Calculate the number of moles for each of the reactants

NH_3: 3.25 g/17 g mol^{-1} = 0.19 moles O_2: 3.5 g/32 g mol^{-1} = 0.11 moles

Step 3 Compare the ratios of what we have versus what the balanced equation tells us we need:

From the equation we can see that 4 moles of NH_3 react with 5 moles of O_2. This tells us that if we have 0.19 moles of NH_3 we need 0.23 moles of O_2.

What we actually have is 0.19 moles of NH_3 reacting with 0.11 moles of O_2.

This tells us that NH_3 was added to excess and O_2 is the limiting factor for the reaction.

H ② Hydrogen reacts with oxygen to produce water: $2H_2(g) + O_2(g) \rightarrow 2H_2O(l)$

If 1 mole of hydrogen is reacted with 1 mole of oxygen, determine the limiting reactant and the reactant in excess by matching the questions on the left to the correct answer on the right. (3 marks, ★★★)

How many moles of water can be produced by 1 mole of H_2?	1
How many moles of water can be produced by 1 mole of O_2?	2
Which is the limiting reactant?	1
How much H_2O is produced in the reaction?	O_2
Which reactant is in excess?	H_2
How many moles of O_2 is used in the reaction?	1

MATHS SKILLS

- To identify the limiting reactant from a chemical equation, work out the number of moles of each reactant and compare this ratio with what is needed by looking at the ratio in the chemical equation for the reaction.

- To convert the ratio in the equation to match the numbers you're told, find the factor by dividing one by the other, depending on the direction you're going. For the worked example above, the ratio is 4:5, which means that for every 4 units of NH_3 you needed 5 units of O_2. You knew the '4' units of NH_3 was 0.19, so to work out how much O_2 needed, simply divide 5 by 4 = 1.25 (i.e. 5 is 1.25 times bigger than 4!) and multiply that by 0.19 = 0.23.

H ③ Copper reacts with oxygen in the air to produce copper(I) oxide, resulting in the green patina that is often seen on copper statues and buildings. The reaction is shown in the equation below:

...... $Cu(s) +$ ...... $O_2(g) \rightarrow$ ...... $Cu_2O(s)$

In an experiment to investigate this reaction, 80 g of copper was reacted with 50 g of oxygen.

a **Balance the equation.** (2 marks, ★★)

b **Calculate the number of moles of the two reactants.** (2 marks, ★★)

c **Identify the limiting reagent and explain your choice.** (2 marks, ★★★)

H ④ Propane is a fuel that is commonly used in portable stoves and increasingly in vehicles, where it is known as liquid petroleum gas (LPG). It combusts in the presence of oxygen. The chemical equation is shown below:

...... $C_3H_8(l) +$ ...... $O_2(g) \rightarrow$ ...... $CO_2(g) +$ ...... $H_2O(g)$

To develop an efficient car engine, a manufacturer is testing mixes with different amounts of oxygen and propane. In this test, 14.8 g of C_3H_8 reacts with 3.44 g of O_2.

a **Balance the equation.** (2 marks, ★★)

b **Calculate the mass of carbon dioxide produced in the reaction.** (2 marks, ★★★)

c **Identify the limiting reagent and suggest how the manufacturer could change the quantities of propane and oxygen to maximise the efficiency of an engine.** (5 marks, ★★★★)

Concentrations in solutions

1. Two solutions are shown in diagrams (1) and (2).

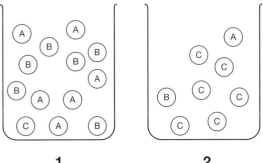

1   2

a **Which of the two solutions has the highest concentration of solute A?**

(1 mark, ★) ....

b **Which of the two solutions has the highest concentration of solute C?**

(1 mark, ★) ....

2. A student dissolved sodium chloride, NaCl, into three beakers of water as shown in the table below.

Test	Amount of solute / g	Volume / dm³
1	5	0.020
2	10	0.025
3	20	0.035

M_r NaCl = 58.5

a **Calculate the concentration of the solute in each of the three tests.** (3 marks, ★★)

Test 1 .... g/dm³

Test 2 .... g/dm³

Test 3 .... g/dm³

b **Calculate the number of moles of solute in each solution.** (3 marks, ★★)

Test 1 .... moles

Test 2 .... moles

Test 3 .... moles

3. The organisers of a swimming competition need to calculate how much cleaning agent to add to the pool to keep it free of harmful microorganisms. The pool contains 2.5×10^6 dm³ water and the instructions on the box of the cleaning agent state that the pool must contain 0.01 mol/dm³ of calcium oxychloride, $Ca(ClO)_2$, before swimming.

a **Determine the M_r of $Ca(ClO)_2$.** (1 mark, ★★) ....

b **Calculate the concentration of $Ca(ClO)_2$ required, in g/mol³.** (1 mark, ★★★) ....

c **Calculate the amount of cleaning agent, in g, that must be added for the pool to contain the correct concentration. Give your answer in standard form.** (3 marks, ★★★★)

....

....

Moles in solution

NAILIT!

- Be careful with your units and orders of magnitude – it is easy to get confused!

- If you're given a volume or concentration with the units cm^3 or mol/cm^3, divide by 1 000!

- Don't forget to write and balance the chemical equation – check the ratio of moles in the equation and change your initial answer accordingly!

H① **A student has 50 cm³ of 5.0 mol/dm⁻³ hydrochloric acid, HCl, which is titrated with sodium hydroxide, NaOH.**

a **How many moles of NaOH are needed to neutralise the HCl? Circle the correct answer.**
(1 mark, ★★)

0.25 moles	4 moles	250 moles	0.1 moles

b **What is the concentration of NaOH if 25 cm³ was used? Circle the correct answer.** (1 mark, ★★)

10 mol/dm⁻³	0.1 mol/dm⁻³	5 mol/dm⁻³	0.5 mol/dm⁻³

H② **An orange juice company wanted to find out the concentration of acid in its juice. The acid in 25.0 cm³ of the orange juice reacted completely with 12.5 cm³ of 0.1 mol/dm³ sodium hydroxide. Calculate the concentration of acid in the orange juice. A previous investigation had shown that 1 mole of the acid reacted with 1 mole of sodium hydroxide to produce 1 mole of salt and water.** (3 marks, ★★★)

....

....

H③ **In a titration, a student finds that 12.6 dm³ of 2.5 mol/dm³ sulfuric acid, H₂SO₄, neutralises 0.025 dm³ of sodium hydroxide, NaOH. Calculate the concentration of the sodium hydroxide.** (3 marks, ★★★★)

....

....

MATHS SKILLS

- The key equation you will use in titration-related questions is $n = c \times V$.

- You need to be able to rearrange that equation – try using equation triangles.

- A common stumbling block for students answering exam questions on this topic is jumbling up the information that is given. One way to avoid this is to create a table that will tell you exactly what is known and what is unknown, like this:

Value	Solution 1 / acid	Solution 2 / alkali
Concentration / c / mol/dm³		
Moles / n / moles		
Volume / V / dm³		

Moles and gas volumes

H 1 **Fill in the gaps to complete the definition of Avogadro's Gas Law.**

At the same temperature and pressure equal .... of different gases contain the

same number of molecules.

This means that under the same conditions, equal volumes of gases have the same number of

.... present.

At .... (20°C) and ...., together known as ...., 1 mole of any

gas occupies a volume of 24 dm³.

atmospheric pressure room temperature room temperature and pressure (RTP)
volumes   gases   moles

H 2 **A car reacts petrol with oxygen, in its engine, at a rate of 6 g of carbon per km. Calculate the volume of carbon dioxide produced in a 12 km journey.** (2 marks, ★★★)

....

....

H 3 **A plant scientist wants to investigate the air conditions in a plant laboratory to understand the optimal conditions for maximum plant growth. The volume of air in the laboratory is 2000 dm³. A meter on the wall measures the percentage composition of the air once a day, as shown in the table below:**

Gas	Per cent in the air (%)
Nitrogen	78.1
Oxygen	20.9
Argon	0.9
Carbon dioxide	0.1

a **Calculate the number of moles of gas in the laboratory.** (1 mark, ★★★)

....

....

b **Calculate the number of moles of carbon dioxide, CO_2, in the laboratory.** (1 mark, ★★★)

....

....

c **Calculate the mass of carbon dioxide, CO_2, in the laboratory.** (1 mark, ★★)

....

Percentage yield and atom economy

(1) TitaniMine, a titanium mining and processing company, are trying to decide which of two methods to use to produce titanium from its ore, TiO_2. The two methods to extract titanium from titanium ore (TiO_2) include:

1 Displacement by magnesium – $TiO_2 + 2Mg \rightarrow Ti + 2MgO$.

2 Electrolysis – $TiO_2 \rightarrow Ti + O_2$

One way that the company could use to compare the two methods is by calculating the atom economy of each reaction.

a Give the formula for working out the atom economy. (1 mark, ★)

b Explain why it is useful for chemists to understand the atom economy for a reaction.
(2 marks, ★★)

....

c Calculate the atom economy for the **two** methods of producing titanium from its ore.
(4 marks, ★★★)

1 ....

....

2 ....

....

d Oxygen is a useful product that can be sold. Explain how this might affect the company's decision in terms of the atom economy. (2 marks, ★★★)

....

....

(2) A student heats 12.5g of calcium carbonate, $CaCO_3$, producing 6.5g of calcium oxide, as shown in the equation below.

$CaCO_3(s) \rightarrow CaO(s) + CO_2(g)$

a Determine the M_r of $CaCO_3$ and CaO. (1 mark, ★)

CaCO₃ .... CaO ....

b What is the correct atom economy of the reaction? Tick **one** box. (2 marks, ★★★)

56%	
44%	
87%	
50%	

c Calculate the maximum theoretical mass of CaO that could be made. (2 marks, ★★)

....

d Calculate the percentage yield of the reaction. (3 marks, ★★★)

....

....

Chemical changes

Metal oxides and the reactivity series

(1) **Magnesium reacts with oxygen to form a white solid.**

   a **Write a word equation for this reaction.** (1 mark, ★★)

....

   b **Write a balanced symbol equation for this reaction.** (2 marks, ★★★)

....

....

   c **In this reaction, magnesium is oxidised. Explain what is meant by oxidation.** (1 mark, ★)

....

....

WORKIT!

More reactive metals will **displace** less reactive metals from metal salts.
This means that the metals swap places in the reaction.

e.g. Sodium + lead oxide → lead + sodium oxide

---

(2) **Use the reactivity series to predict the outcome of the following reactions.**
(4 marks, ★★)

   a **Aluminium + lead chloride →** ....

   b **Silver + copper oxide →** ....

   c **Calcium + zinc nitrate →** ....

   d **Iron chloride + copper →** ....

(3) **A student has an unknown metal, X, and carries out some experiments in order to determine its reactivity. The student's results are in the table below.**

1	X + copper sulfate solution	A red/orange solid is formed
2	X + sodium sulfate solution	No reaction
3	X + magnesium sulfate	A silvery grey solid is produced
4	X + hydrochloric acid	X dissolves vigorously and a gas is produced

Metal	Reactivity
Copper	
Sodium	1
Magnesium	
X	

   a **Use the student's results to place the metals in order of reactivity, with 1 being the most reactive and 4 being the least reactive. The most reactive is done for you.** (2 marks, ★★)

   b **What is the name of the red/orange solid formed in experiment 1?** (1 mark, ★★★)

....

Extraction of metals and reduction

(1) **Magnesium cannot be extracted from its ore by heating with carbon. Explain why.** (1 mark, ★★)

....

(2) **Why does gold not need to be extracted from an ore?** (1 mark, ★★)

....

(3) **Copper is extracted from its ore by heating it with carbon. One of the copper compounds found in copper ore is copper oxide.**

a **Write a word equation for this reaction.** (2 marks, ★★★)

....

b **Which substance is oxidised in this reaction?** (1 mark, ★★)

....

(4) **Iron is extracted from its ore in the blast furnace (figure 1). The iron ore, which contains mostly iron(III) oxide, is mixed with carbon and heated to around 1 500°C. The following reaction takes place.**

Iron(III) oxide + carbon → iron + carbon dioxide

a **What type of reaction is this?** (1 mark, ★★)

....

....

b **Balance the symbol equation for this reaction below.**
(2 marks, ★★★★)

.... $Fe_2O_3(s)$ + ... $C(s)$ → .... $Fe(l)$ + ... $CO_2(g)$

c **How can you tell from the equation that the reaction is carried out at a high temperature?** (1 mark, ★★★)

....

....

d **Why can carbon be used to extract iron from its ore?**
(1 mark, ★★)

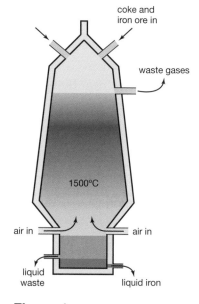

Figure 1

....

....

e **Using the reactivity series, predict another element which could be used to extract iron from its ore. Suggest why this element is not used in practice.** (2 marks, ★★★)

....

....

....

The reactions of acids

1. State **one similarity** and **one difference** between bases and alkalis. (2 marks, ★★★)

   ....

   ....

   ....

2. Choose **two** chemicals from the table that could be used to make the following salts.
   (3 marks, ★★)

   a **Sodium chloride** ....

   b **Potassium nitrate** ....

   c **Copper sulfate** ....

Copper chloride	Sodium hydroxide	Sulfuric acid
Nitric acid	Chlorine	Potassium carbonate
Sodium sulfate	Hydrochloric acid	Copper oxide

3. **Magnesium oxide and magnesium carbonate are both white solids that will react with dilute acids, including hydrochloric acid, HCl.**

   A student adds HCl to separate portions of magnesium oxide and magnesium carbonate and makes observations.

   a **State one observation that the two reactions would have in common.** (1 mark, ★★)

   ....

   b **State one observation that would be different.** (1 mark, ★★)

   ....

   c **Write the word equation for the reaction between magnesium oxide and hydrochloric acid.** (1 mark, ★★)

   ....

   d **What is the formula for magnesium carbonate?** (1 mark, ★★★) ....

4. Write symbol equations for these reactions, including state symbols. (6 marks, ★★★★)

   a **Magnesium + hydrochloric acid** ....

   b **Lithium oxide + sulfuric acid** ....

   c **Copper(II) oxide + hydrochloric acid** ....

5. **The reaction between calcium and hydrochloric acid is a redox reaction. This means that both oxidation and reduction take place at the same time.**

   a **Write an ionic equation for this reaction. Include state symbols.** (3 marks, ★★★★★)

   ....

   b **State which species is oxidised and which species is reduced.** (2 marks, ★★★★)

   ....

The preparation of soluble salts

(1) **A sample of copper sulfate can be formed by reacting together solid copper carbonate and dilute sulfuric acid.**

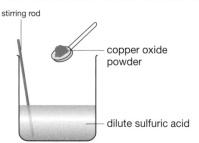

stirring rod

copper oxide powder

dilute sulfuric acid

NAILIT!

The preparation of soluble salts can be summarised as follows:

• Heat acid

• Add insoluble base until no more reacts

• Filter excess base

• Allow solution to crystallise

This is the basic method regardless of which type of base is used!

a **Complete the word equation for this reaction.** (1 mark, ★★)

Copper carbonate + sulfuric acid → copper sulfate + ... + ...

b **State two observations that would be seen during this reaction.** (2 marks, ★★)

....

c **The copper carbonate needs to be added until it is in excess. Explain why this is necessary.** (1 mark, ★★)

....

d **How is the excess copper carbonate removed?** (1 mark, ★)

....

e **State another chemical that reacts with sulfuric acid to form copper sulfate.** (1 mark, ★★)

....

f **When soluble salts are prepared in this way, the percentage yield is generally less than 100%. Suggest one reason why.** (1 mark, ★★)

....

(2) **A soluble salt is formed in the reaction between calcium and nitric acid.**

Calcium + nitric acid → calcium nitrate + hydrogen

a **Write a balanced symbol equation for this reaction, including state symbols.** (3 marks, ★★★★)

....

b **A student carried out the experiment above and made 2.6 g of calcium nitrate. If the theoretical yield is 3.0 g, what is the percentage yield? Quote your answer to one decimal place.** (2 marks, ★★★)

....

(3) **On a separate piece of paper, describe how to make a pure, dry sample of zinc chloride. Include an equation and a full equipment list.** (6 marks, ★★★★)

Oxidation and reduction in terms of electrons

(1) **Magnesium reacts with a solution of copper(II) chloride to form a solution of magnesium chloride and solid copper.**

 a **Write an ionic equation, including state symbols, for this reaction.** (3 marks, ★★★★)

 ....

 b **Which species is oxidised and which is reduced?** (1 mark, ★★★)

 ....

WORKIT!

Step 1 Write a balanced symbol equation, including state symbols.

$$Mg(s) + CuCl_2(aq) \rightarrow MgCl_2(aq) + Cu(s)$$

Step 2 Any aqueous solution will split up into its ions. Rewrite the equation to show this.

$$Mg(s) + Cu^{2+}(aq) + 2Cl^-(aq) \rightarrow Mg^{2+}(aq) + 2Cl^-(aq) + Cu(s)$$

Step 3 Cancel out any species that appear on both sides of the equation. These are **spectator ions** and don't take part in the reaction.

$$Mg(s) + Cu^{2+}(aq) + \cancel{2Cl^-(aq)} \rightarrow Mg^{2+}(aq) + \cancel{2Cl^-(aq)} + Cu(s)$$

Step 4 Rewrite the equation with the remaining ions.

$$Mg(s) + Cu^{2+}(aq) \rightarrow Mg^{2+}(aq) + Cu(s)$$

Step 5 The Mg has lost electrons and formed a positive ion, so according to OILRIG, it has been oxidised. The Cu^{2+} has gained electrons and has therefore been reduced.

(2) **Write ionic equations for the following reactions. In each case, state which species has been oxidised and which has been reduced.**

 a **Zinc(II) nitrate reacts with magnesium to form magnesium nitrate and solid zinc.**
 (4 marks, ★★★★★)

 ....

 b **Sodium reacts with a solution of zinc(II) chloride to form a solution of sodium chloride and solid zinc.**
 (4 marks, ★★★★★)

 ....

 c **Silver(I) sulfate reacts with copper to form copper(II) sulfate and silver metal.** (4 marks, ★★★★★)

 ....

 d **Calcium reacts with a solution of iron(III) chloride to form solid iron and a solution of calcium chloride.** (4 marks, ★★★★★)

 ....

NAILIT!

Writing ionic equations is tricky and you need to make sure you can write formulae correctly. You cannot always use the periodic table to work out the charges on metal ions, as the transition metals often form more than one ion. Here are some common ones.

Zinc – Zn^{2+} Iron(II) – Fe^{2+}

Copper – Cu^{2+} Iron(III) – Fe^{3+}

Silver – Ag^+

pH scale and neutralisation

(1) **Match each solution with its correct pH value and colour that universal indicator would change to. The first one is done for you.** (4 marks, ★★)

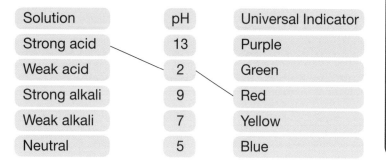

Solution	pH	Universal Indicator
Strong acid	13	Purple
Weak acid	2	Green
Strong alkali	9	Red
Weak alkali	7	Yellow
Neutral	5	Blue

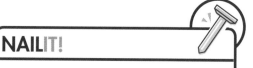

NAILIT!

All neutralisation reactions between an acid and an alkali can be simply represented by this ionic equation:

$H^+(aq) + OH^-(aq) \rightarrow H_2O(l)$

Always include this if you are asked about neutralisation; equations are an excellent way of gaining marks.

(2) **State the name of the ion that causes solutions to be alkaline.** (1 mark, ★) ....

(3) **State the formula of the ion that causes solutions to be acidic.** (1 mark, ★) ....

(4) **Which of these solutions has the greatest concentration of H⁺ ions? Tick one box.**
(1 mark, ★★)

pH 3	☐
pH 1	☐

(5) **Which of these solutions has the lowest concentration of OH⁻ ions? Tick one box.**
(1 mark, ★★)

pH 14	☐
pH 12	☐

(6) **Potassium sulfate, K_2SO_4, can be produced in the reaction between sulfuric acid and an alkali.**

a **State the name of the alkali that could be used.** (1 mark, ★)

....

b **Write a symbol equation for this reaction.** (2 marks, ★★★★)

....

c **Write the ionic equation for this reaction.** (1 mark, ★★★)

....

(7) **Ammonia gas, NH_3, forms an alkaline solution when dissolved in water. Suggest the formulae of the two ions formed.** (2 marks, ★★★★★)

....

H

Strong and weak acids

WORKIT!

Hydrochloric acid, HCl, is a strong acid and ethanoic acid, CH_3COOH, is a weak acid. Write equations to show how they ionise in aqueous solution. (2 marks, ★★★)

Strong acids completely ionise (split up into ions) when they are in solution.

$HCl(aq) \rightarrow H^+(aq) + Cl^-(aq)$

Weak acids only partially ionise when they are in solution. This is represented by using the reversible arrow ($\rightleftharpoons$) in the equation.

$CH_3COOH(aq) \rightleftharpoons CH_3COO^-(aq) + H^+(aq)$

H(1) **Write equations to show how the following acids ionise in solution.** (3 marks, ★★★)

a **Nitric acid, HNO_3 (strong acid)**

....

b **Methanoic acid, HCOOH (weak acid)**

....

c **Sulfuric acid, H_2SO_4 (strong acid)**

....

H(2) **Explain the difference between a weak acid and a dilute acid.** (2 marks, ★★★)

....

....

....

H(3) **An acid with pH 3 has a hydrogen ion concentration of $0.001\,mol/dm^3$.**

a **Express this value in standard form.** (1 mark, ★★★)

....

b **What is the hydrogen ion concentration of an acid with a pH of 1? Express your answer in standard form.** (3 marks, ★★★★★)

....

....

....

 **NAILIT!**

Strong and concentrated do not mean the same thing!

Concentration refers to how much of a solute is dissolved in a solution. More solute means a **higher** concentration.

If an acid is strong, this means that it completely splits or **dissociates** into its ions in solution.

Electrolysis

① **Label the diagram choosing the correct words from the box below.** (3 marks, ★★)

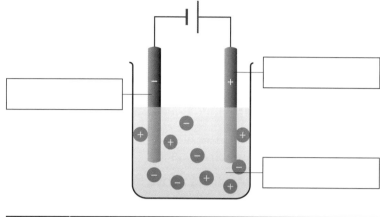

| cathode | electrolyte | electroplating | anode |

② **Why can ionic compounds conduct electricity when melted or in solution but not when they are solids?** (2 marks, ★★)

....

③ **Predict the products formed when these compounds undergo electrolysis.** (3 marks, ★★)

a **Molten zinc chloride** ....

b **Molten silver iodide** ....

c **Molten copper oxide** ....

④ **Molten lead bromide undergoes electrolysis to form lead and bromine.**

a **Complete the half equations for this reaction.** (2 marks, ★★★)

• $Pb^{2+} +$ .... $\rightarrow Pb$

• $2Br^- \rightarrow Br_2 +$ ....

b **What is oxidised and what is reduced?** (1 mark, ★★★)

....

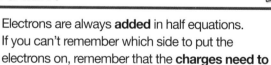

DO IT!

Practise writing half equations for simple ionic compounds.

Step 1 Use the charges on ions to write a formula, e.g. K^+ and Cl^- forms KCl.

Step 2 Write out the half equations:

$K^+ \rightarrow K$

$Cl^- \rightarrow Cl_2$

Step 3 Balance any atoms:

$K^+ \rightarrow K$ *already balanced*

$2Cl^- \rightarrow Cl_2$ *2Cl- needed*

Step 4 Add electrons to balance the charges.

$K^+ + e^- \rightarrow K$

$2Cl^- \rightarrow Cl_2 + 2e^-$

NAILIT!

Electrons are always **added** in half equations. If you can't remember which side to put the electrons on, remember that the **charges need to be balanced**.

e.g. During electrolysis of NaCl, Na^+ ions form Na metal.

$Na^+ \rightarrow Na$

There is a **positive** charge on the **left hand side**, which means that **one electron** needs to be added to the **right hand side** to balance the charge.

$Na^+ \rightarrow Na + e^-$

The electrolysis of aqueous solutions

(1) **State the products formed when the following aqueous solutions undergo electrolysis.**
(4 marks, ★★★)

a **Copper chloride** ....

b **Potassium bromide** ....

c **Zinc sulfate** ....

d **Sodium carbonate** ....

(2) **When a solution of sodium chloride undergoes electrolysis, two gases are formed at the electrodes.**

a **The gas formed at the cathode is hydrogen. Complete the half equation for this reaction.** (2 marks, ★★★)

.... H^+ + ... → .... H_2

b **What is the name of the gas formed at the anode? Write a half equation to show how it is formed.** (3 marks, ★★★★)

....

....

> **NAILIT!**
>
> Learn these rules to predict the products of the electrolysis of aqueous solutions.
>
> | Positive ion | Cathode |
> | --- | --- |
> | Copper and below in reactivity series | Metal |
> | Anything above hydrogen in reactivity series | Hydrogen |
>
> | Negative ion | Anode |
> | --- | --- |
> | Chloride, bromide, iodide | Halogen |
> | Sulfate, nitrate, carbonate | Oxygen |

(3) **A solution of lithium iodide, LiI, undergoes electrolysis.**

a **This solution contains a mixture of ions, including iodide, I^-, ions. State the other three ions present.** (2 marks, ★★★)

....

b **Explain what happens to the iodide ions during electrolysis.** (3 marks, ★★★★)

....

....

c **What is the name of the remaining solution?** (1 mark, ★★★★) ....

(4) **When a solution of copper sulfate undergoes electrolysis, one of the products formed is oxygen.**

a **Where is oxygen formed; the anode or the cathode?** (1 mark, ★) ....

b **Write a half equation to show the formation of oxygen.** (3 marks, ★★★★★)

....

....

The extraction of metals using electrolysis

(1) **Aluminium is extracted from its ore by electrolysis. The most common aluminium ore is called bauxite and this is purified to produce aluminium oxide, Al_2O_3. The aluminium oxide is heated to around 950 °C and dissolved in another aluminium compound called cryolite. The mixture then undergoes electrolysis and forms aluminium and oxygen.**

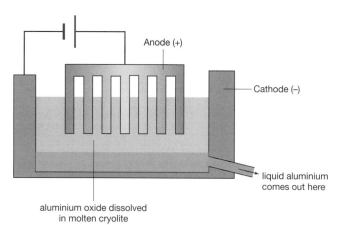

Anode (+)

Cathode (–)

liquid aluminium comes out here

aluminium oxide dissolved in molten cryolite

> **NAILIT!**
>
> This topic links with the **reactivity series** and **structure and bonding**. Make sure you can remember **why** ionic compounds can conduct electricity.

a **Aluminium oxide has a high melting point. Use your ideas about structure and bonding to explain why.** (2 marks, ★★★)

....

....

b **Why does the aluminium oxide need to be heated?** (1 mark, ★★)

....

c **Why is cryolite added to the aluminium oxide?** (2 marks, ★★★)

....

d **The reaction that takes place at the anode is replaced with: $2O^{2-} \rightarrow O_2 + 4e^-$**

This equation shows oxidation. Explain why. (1 mark, ★★)

....

e **Aluminium is produced at the cathode. Write a half equation to show this reaction.**
(2 marks, ★★★)

....

f **The graphite anodes need to be frequently replaced. Use an equation to explain why.**
(2 marks, ★★★)

....

....

g **Aluminium was not discovered until around 200 years ago, yet there is evidence to suggest that iron was used by humans over 7000 years ago. Suggest why it took a long time for aluminium to be discovered.** (1 mark, ★★)

....

Practical investigation into the electrolysis of aqueous solutions

Hypothesis: The product produced at the cathode when an aqueous solution undergoes hydrolysis depends on the reactivity of the metal in the salt solution.

A student carries out the following experiment with 4 different metal salt solutions, all of which have a concentration of $1\,mol/dm^3$. The salt solutions are:

- **Iron(III) chloride, $FeCl_3(aq)$**
- **Sodium chloride, $NaCl(aq)$**
- **Copper chloride, $CuCl_2(aq)$**
- **Magnesium chloride, $MgCl_2(aq)$**

Method

- **Measure out $100\,cm^3$ of iron(III) chloride solution in a measuring cylinder and pour into a beaker.**
- **Place two inert electrodes into the beaker and attach to a power pack.**
- **Set voltage to 4V, switch on the power pack and observe the product formed at the cathode.**
- **If a gas is produced, test to see if it is hydrogen.**
- **Repeat for the remaining salt solutions.**

(1) a **In the table below, state the variables in this experiment.** (4 marks, ★★★)

Independent variable	Dependent variable	Control variables

b **Explain why this experiment is a fair test.** (1 mark, ★)

....

(2) **What is the test for hydrogen gas?** (2 marks, ★★) ....

....

(3) a **In the table below, predict the products that will be formed at the cathode.** (2 marks, ★★★)

Salt solution	Product produced at the cathode
$FeCl_3$	
$NaCl$	
$CuCl_2$	
$MgCl_2$	

b **Explain why you made this prediction.** (2 marks, ★★★)

....

(4) **All four solutions will produce the same product at the anode. Name this gas, and describe a test to identify it.** (2 marks, ★★★)

....

....

Titrations

(1) **The results from a titration are shown below.**

	Rough	1	2	3
Final volume/cm³	15.60	30.50	45.85	14.80
Initial volume/cm³	0.00	15.60	30.50	0.00
Titre/cm³	15.60			

a **Calculate the titre values for experiments 1, 2 and 3.** (2 marks, ★★)

b **Calculate the mean titre.** (2 marks, ★★★) ....

c **How many times should a titration be carried out?** (1 mark, ★★★) ....

H(2) **Work out the unknown concentrations and volumes in the table below.** (3 marks, ★★★)

The equation for the reaction is: NaOH + HCl → NaCl + H₂O

Volume NaOH (cm³)	Concentration NaOH (mol/dm³)	Volume HCl (cm³)	Concentration HCl (mol/dm³)
25.00	0.1	25.00	0.1
25.00	0.1	50.00	
12.50	0.2		0.1
20.00	0.5	10.00	

H(3) **A student has a solution of sodium hydroxide, NaOH, and a solution of nitric acid, HNO₃.**

On a separate piece of paper, describe how they could carry out an experiment to find out the exact volumes of these solutions that would react together. Include an equipment list. (6 marks, ★★★)

H(4) **In a titration, 25 cm³ of 0.1 mol/dm³ of sodium hydroxide, NaOH, reacts with 21.60 cm³ of nitric acid, HNO₃. NaOH + HNO₃ → NaNO₃ + H₂O**

Calculate the concentration of nitric acid in:

a **mol/cm³** (3 marks, ★★★★★) ....

b **g/dm³, [H = 1, N = 14, O = 16]** (2 marks, ★★★) ....

H(5) **In another titration, 25 cm³ of 0.2 mol/dm³ of potassium hydroxide, KOH, reacts with 14.50 cm³ of sulfuric acid, H₂SO₄.** .... KOH + ... H₂SO₄ → .... K₂SO₄ + ... H₂O

a **Balance the equation for this reaction.** (1 mark, ★★)

b **Calculate the concentration of the sulfuric acid in**

i **mol/dm³** (3 marks, ★★★★★) ....

ii **g/dm³, [H = 1, S = 32, O = 16]** (2 marks, ★★★) ....

Energy changes

Exothermic and endothermic reactions

1. Explain what happens to the temperature of the surroundings during 'endothermic' and 'exothermic' reactions. (2 marks, ★)

   a **Endothermic** ....

   ....

   b **Exothermic** ....

   ....

2. A student set up an experiment as shown in the image below. The initial temperature of solution was 23.7°C. At the end of the reaction the temperature was 15.4°C.

   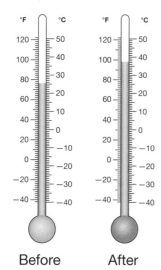

   a **Calculate the temperature change of the reaction and state whether the reaction is exothermic or endothermic.** (3 marks, ★★)

   ....

   ....

   b **Another student repeated the experiment with different reactants. They recorded the temperature at the start and at the end of the reaction as shown below.**

   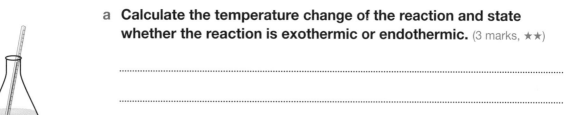

   Before   After

   i **Calculate the temperature change of the reaction.** (2 marks, ★★)

   ....

   ii **State whether the reaction is endothermic or exothermic.** (1 mark, ★★)

   ....

NAILIT!

Exothermic reactions include combustion (burning) reactions, most oxidation reactions and neutralisation reactions.

Endothermic reactions include *thermal decomposition* (breaking up of a compound using heat) and the reaction of citric acid with sodium hydrogen carbonate.

Practical investigation into the variables that affect temperature changes in chemical reactions

(1) **A student is comparing the temperature change in the reaction of iron with oxygen. She set up the experiment as shown in the diagram below.**

a **Label the diagram to identify the equipment the student used.** (4 marks, ★)

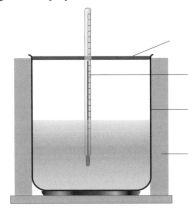

b **Suggest why the student wrapped the calorimeter in wool.** (2 marks, ★★)

....

....

The results of the experiment are shown below.

	Iron filings	Iron ball bearings	A large piece of iron
Initial temperature / °C	24.2	23.9	24.1
Final temperature / °C	60.1	37.3	24.3

c **What conclusions could be made from these results?** (2 marks, ★★)

....

....

d **Explain why it is important that the student kept the volume of air the same in all three tests.** (2 marks, ★★★)

....

....

(2) **On a separate piece of paper, describe how you would set up an experiment to investigate how the concentration of hydrochloric acid affects the temperature change during its reaction with calcium carbonate.** (6 marks, ★★★★)

Your answer should include:

- **an explanation for your choice of equipment**

- **the hypothesis you will be testing**

- **a prediction of what you think will happen and why**

- **how you would ensure a fair test**

- **how you would record your results.**

NAILIT!

If asked why a student has kept a variable the same, it is usually not enough to simply say "to make it a fair test" – you will typically be expected to explain what could happen if that variable was changed. For example, if a student is investigating the effect of particle size, it is important to keep the concentration the same, because increasing concentration can increase the rate of reaction and so would also affect the temperature change.

Reaction profiles

NAILIT!

One way to help you remember the energy changes in endo- and exothermic relations is to remember **ex**othermic involves the **ex**it of energy to the surroundings – surrounding temperatures will increase, but the amount of energy in the products will reduce. The reverse is true for endothermic reactions.

(1) **Fill the gaps to complete the sentence about reaction profiles for endothermic and exothermic reactions.** (4 marks, ★)

A .... shows how the energy changes from reactants to products.

In a reaction profile for an .... reaction the products are lower in energy than the reactants because .... is released to the surroundings during the reaction.

In a reaction profile for an .... reaction the .... are higher in energy than the .... because energy is taken in from the .... during the reaction.

Chemical reactions occur when reacting particles collide with enough energy to react. This energy is called the .... (Ea).

| surroundings | energy | products | reaction profile |
| reactants | activation energy | endothermic | exothermic |

(2) **A student reacts barium hydroxide, $Ba(OH)_2.8H_2O(s)$, with ammonium chloride, $NH_4Cl(s)$, as shown in the balanced equation below:**

$$Ba(OH)_2.8H_2O(s) + 2NH_4Cl(s) \rightarrow 2NH_3(g) + 10H_2O(l) + BaCl_2(s)$$

The student predicts that the reaction will be exothermic.

a **Use the reaction profile diagram below to suggest whether the student's prediction is correct. Explain your answer.** (3 marks, ★★★)

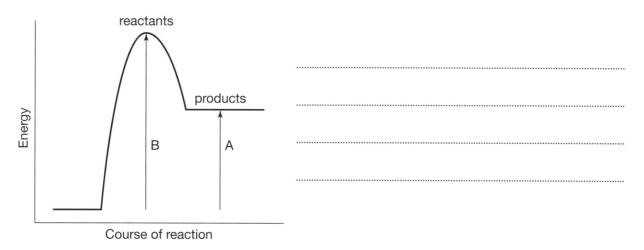

....

....

....

....

b **Identify what is shown on the diagram by labels A and B.** (2 marks, ★★)

i **A** ....

ii **B** ....

c **On a separate piece of paper, draw a diagram to show how a catalyst might change the reaction profile.** (2 marks, ★★★)

The energy changes of reactions

H(1) 1 mole of hydrogen and 1 mole of chlorine react to form 2 moles of hydrogen chloride gas, as shown below.

Bond	Bond energy (kJ per mol)
H–H	436
Cl–Cl	243
H–Cl	432

H–H + Cl–Cl → 2 × (H–Cl)

a Calculate the amount of energy required to break both the H-H and Cl-Cl bonds. (2 marks, ★★)

H-H: ....

Cl-Cl: .... Sum (bond breaking): ....

b Calculate the amount of energy released as the H-Cl bonds are formed. (2 marks, ★★)

....

c Suggest whether the reaction is exothermic or endothermic. (1 mark, ★★★)

....

d Calculate the energy change of the reaction. (1 mark, ★★★)

....

H(2) 2 moles of hydrogen bromide produce 1 mole of hydrogen and bromine gas.

$2HBr(g) \rightarrow H_2(g) + Br_2(g)$

Bond	Bond energy (kJ per mol)
H–Br	366
Br–Br	193
H–Cl	432

a Draw the bonds present in the molecules. (3 marks, ★★)

b Calculate the energy change of the reaction and identify whether the reaction is endothermic or exothermic. (★★★★, 3 marks)

....

....

....

Chemical cells and fuel cells

1 A student put strips of copper and zinc into a lemon and created a circuit using two wires and an **LED** bulb, as shown in the picture below.

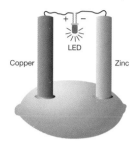

a **Identify the most reactive metal in the circuit.** (1 mark, ★)

....

NAIL**IT!**

Can you come up with a mnemonic to help you remember the reactivity series of metals?

b **Identify the electrolyte in the circuit.** (1 mark, ★) c **Draw an arrow on the picture to show the flow of electrons.** (1 mark, ★★)

....

2 A battery company produces 9 volt batteries by connecting 1.5V cells in series. Calculate the number of cells in the battery. (2 marks, ★★)

....

....

3 A significant amount of research in battery technology has involved hydrogen fuel cells which may in future replace traditional chemical cells and the combustion of fossil fuels to provide the energy we need for our electronic devices and cars.

a **Identify the reaction that occurs that produces water from hydrogen.** (1 mark, ★★)

....

b **Discuss the advantages and disadvantages of hydrogen fuel cells as a replacement for chemical cells.** (6 marks, ★★★)

....

....

....

....

....

....

H c **Write the half equations for the electrode reactions in the hydrogen fuel cell.** (2 marks, ★★)

....

....

 STRETCHIT!

The two half equations for a zinc-copper cell are shown below.

$Zn(s) \rightarrow Zn^{2+}(aq) + 2e^-$

$Cu \leftarrow Cu^{2+}(aq) + 2e$

Try writing the half equations for a cell that uses the reaction:

$Ni(s) + 2Fe^{3+} \rightarrow Ni^{2+} + 2Fe^{2+}$

Rates of reaction and equilibrium

Ways to follow a chemical reaction

1. A student wants to investigate how the size of marble chips affects the rate of reaction with hydrochloric acid. The chemical equation for the reaction is:

$$CaCO_3(s) + 2HCl(aq) \rightarrow CO_2(g) + H_2O(l) + CaCl_2(s)$$

   a Identify the independent variable in this experiment. (1 mark, ★)

   ....

   b What else does the student need to record to be able to calculate the **rate** of the reaction? (1 mark, ★)

   ....

   c Suggest what the student could use as the dependent variable in the experiment. **Explain your answer.** (2 marks, ★★)

   ....

   d Suggest what variables the student would need to control to ensure the investigation was a fair test. (2 marks, ★★)

   ....

2. In an experiment to investigate the effect of concentration on the rate of reaction, a student is given sodium thiosulfate ($Na_2S_2O_3$) and $2\,mol/dm^3$ hydrochloric acid (HCl). The chemical equation for the reaction is:

$$2HCl(aq) + Na_2S_2O_3(aq) \rightarrow 2NaCl(aq) + SO_2(g) + S(s) + H_2O(l)$$

   The student marks a sheet of paper with an X and places it under the flask in which the reaction will take place.

   a Suggest what the student is using to identify the progress of the reaction. (1 mark, ★)

   ....

   b Identify the independent variable in the experiment. (1 mark, ★)

   ....

   c What variables should be controlled to ensure a fair test? (2 marks, ★★)

   ....

   d Explain how this experiment could be improved to reduce inaccuracy. (2 marks, ★★★)

   ....

3. On a separate piece of paper, describe how you would use the equipment listed below to investigate how the concentration of hydrochloric acid affects the rate of its reaction with magnesium. Explain how you will ensure a fair test. (6 marks, ★★★)

   - magnesium ribbon
   - hydrochloric acid
   - safety goggles
   - conical flask
   - bung and delivery tube to fit conical flask
   - trough or plastic washing-up bowl
   - measuring cylinder
   - clamp stand, boss and clamp
   - stop clock

Calculating the rate of reaction

(1) **Describe how you could calculate the rate of a reaction from the amount of product formed.** (1 mark, ★)

....

(2) **For each of the graphs below, describe what is shown in terms of the rate of reaction.**
(4 marks, ★★)

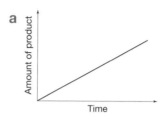

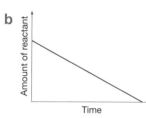

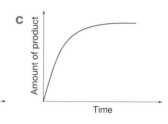

....

(3) **In a reaction between magnesium and hydrochloric acid, hydrogen gas is given off. The volume of hydrogen was recorded every 10 seconds, as shown in the table.**

Time/s	0	10	20	30	40	50	60	70	80	90	100	110	120
Volume of H_2/cm³	0	21	39	55	67	76	84	91	95	97	98	99	99

a **Write a balanced equation for the reaction.** (1 mark, ★)

....

b **Calculate the mean rate of the reaction in cm³/second.** (2 marks, ★★)

....

c **On a piece of graph paper draw a graph of the results.** (3 marks, ★★)

d **Draw a tangent to the curves on your graph at 30s, 60s and 90s.** (3 marks, ★★★)

NAILIT!

To calculate the rate of reaction you can either use the amount of reactant used:

$$\text{Mean rate of reaction} = \frac{\text{Amount of reactant used up}}{\text{Time taken}}$$

Or the product formed:

$$\text{Mean rate of reaction} = \frac{\text{Amount of product formed}}{\text{Time taken}}$$

H e **Calculate the rate of reaction at 30s, 60s and 90s from the tangents of your graph.**
(3 marks, ★★★★)

....

H f **Calculate the rate of the reaction in moles/second of hydrogen gas produced at 30s and 60s.** (4 marks, ★★★★)

....

....

The effect of concentration on reaction rate and the effect of pressure on the rate of gaseous reactions

(1) **Fill the gaps to complete the sentence.** (3 marks, ★)

For a reaction to happen, particles must .... with sufficient .... The minimum amount of .... that particles must have for a specific reaction is known as the .... The rate of a reaction can be increased by increasing the .... of collisions and increasing the .... of collisions.

frequency activation energy energy collide	(some words are used more than once)

(2) **A student planned to investigate the effect of concentration on the rate of reaction. The student predicted that the rate of reaction would increase as the concentration increased.**

Give two reasons the student's prediction is correct. Tick two boxes. (2 marks, ★★)

There are more particles.	
The particles have more energy.	
The particles have a larger surface area.	
The frequency of successful collisions increases.	
The particles have greater mass.	

(3) **A student investigated how pressure affects the rate of reaction between two gases.**

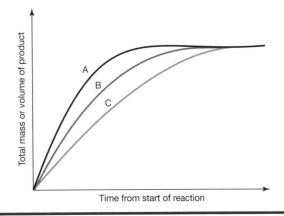

a **Identify which curve represents the lowest pressure.** (1 mark, ★★) ....

b **Identify which curve represents the highest pressure.** (1 mark, ★★) ....

NAILIT!

Remember that concentration is the number of moles of a substance per unit of volume.

- If you increase the moles but keep the volume the same, you've increased the concentration. Increasing the concentration means it is more likely that the particles will collide successfully.

- Similarly, if you keep the same number of moles but decrease the volume, you've also increased the concentration.

- Concentration = number of moles/volume

For gases, increasing pressure has the same effect – and you can increase the pressure by reducing the size of the container or increasing the number of particles.

(4) Another student investigated the reaction between marble chips and hydrochloric acid. The student collected the carbon dioxide, CO_2, given off and recorded the amount at intervals of 10 s. The results are shown below.

Time (s)	0	10	20	30	40	50	60	70
Volume of CO_2 (cm³)	0.0	1.4	2.4	2.9	3.5	3.9	4.1	4.1

a **Plot this data on a graph, including a line of best fit.** (3 marks, ★★)

b **Use your graph to describe how the rate of the reaction changes with time.** (2 marks, ★★)

....

c **The reaction eventually stops. Pick the correct explanation for this. Tick one box.** (1 mark, ★★★)

The catalyst has been used up	
The particles do not have enough energy	
The pressure reduces	
One (or more) of the reactants has been used up	
The temperature reduces	

d **Sketch on your graph what you would expect to see if the concentration of hydrochloric acid was halved.** (2 marks, ★★★★)

e **Explain, in terms of particles, the reason for this difference.** (3 marks, ★★★★)

....

....

....

Rates of reaction – the effect of surface area

(1) A student is investigating how surface area affects the rate of the reaction of calcium carbonate, $CaCO_3$, and hydrochloric acid, HCl.

A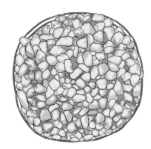

B

    a Identify which sample of calcium carbonate has the larger surface area. (1 mark, ★) ....

    b Predict which you think will give the fastest rate of reaction. (1 mark, ★★) ....

    c Explain, in terms of particles, your answer to (b). (2 marks, ★★)

    ....

    ....

    d Marshmallows are made primarily of sugar. They are produced by mixing finely powdered sugar, water, gelling agent and flavourings. When exposed to a flame, marshmallows burn slowly.

        Explain why factories producing marshmallows often have strict rules in place to prevent explosive fires. (2 marks, ★★★)

        ....

        ....

    ....

(2) A pharmaceutical company produces medicine in the form of effervescent tablets that dissolve in water. As the tablet dissolves, carbon dioxide bubbles are produced. Following feedback from patients, the company want to investigate how they can reduce the time it takes for the medicine to dissolve.

    a Suggest how the company could vary the surface area of the tablets. (2 marks, ★★)

    ....

    b The company recorded the loss of mass as a tablet dissolved in a beaker of water, as shown in the graph. Sketch onto the graph what you would expect to find if the tablet was crushed into powder. (1 mark, ★★★)

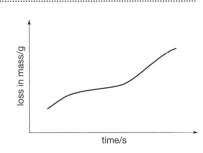

    c Suggest another method the company could use in their experiment to follow the rate of the reaction. (2 marks, ★★)

    ....

    ....

The effects of changing the temperature and adding a catalyst

1 A student wanted to investigate the effect of temperature on the rate of a reaction. The student put $10\,cm^3$ of sodium thiosulfate, $Na_2S_2O_3$, in a beaker with $10\,cm^3$ of hydrochloric acid and recorded the time it took for a cross to become obscured. The student predicted that the rate of reaction would increase with increasing temperature.

a Give **two** reasons the student's prediction is correct. (2 marks, ★)

....

b At 20°C the student found that it took 40 s for the cross to disappear. Predict how long it would take for the cross to disappear at 40°C. (2 marks, ★★)

....

2 The Haber process produces ammonia, NH_3, by passing nitrogen and hydrogen over iron.

a What is iron used as in the reaction? (1 mark, ★★)

....

b Explain how iron increases the rate of the reaction. (2 marks, ★★★)

....

c Complete the diagram below by labelling the line representing the reaction with and without iron. (2 marks, ★★★)

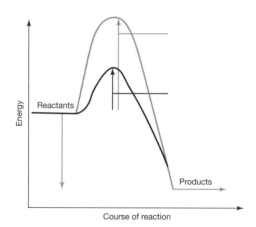

3 Hydrogen peroxide, H_2O_2, decomposes at room temperature to produce water and oxygen, as shown in the balanced equation below:

$$2H_2O_2\,(aq) \rightarrow 2H_2O(l) + O_2\,(g)$$

a How could you measure the rate of the reaction? (1 mark, ★★★)

....

b Manganese oxide, MnO_2, can be used as a catalyst to increase the rate of decomposition of hydrogen peroxide. Catalase is an enzyme found in the liver where it also increases the decomposition of hydrogen peroxide. On a separate piece of paper explain how you would set up an experiment to investigate which is more effective at increasing the rate of decomposition. State how you would ensure a fair test in your answer. (4 marks, ★★★★)

An investigation into how changing the concentration affects the rate of reaction

① You are given sodium thiosulfate ($Na_2S_2O_3$) and hydrochloric acid (HCl) and asked to investigate how changing the concentration of sodium thiosulfate or hydrochloric acid affects the rate of reaction. The chemical equation for the reaction is:

..........HCl(aq) + ...$Na_2S_2O_3$(aq) → ....NaCl(aq) + ...SO_2(g) + ...S(s) + ...H_2O(l)

a **Balance the equation.** (1 mark, ★)

b **Suggest a suitable hypothesis for the investigation.** (1 mark, ★★)

....

c **Make a prediction for your investigation. Explain your prediction.** (3 marks, ★★★)

....

....

d **Describe how you would use different equipment to test your hypothesis. Suggest how you would ensure a fair test.** (4 marks, ★★★)

....

....

....

....

e **Explain how a change in temperature could affect your results.**

(2 marks, ★★★)

....

....

....

....

f **Evaluate two different methods you could use to measure the progress of the reaction.** (4 marks, ★★★)

....

....

....

....

MATHS SKILLS

- You should be comfortable developing hypotheses and making predictions.
- The hypotheses in these reactions will always be that increasing concentration of a reactant increases the reaction rate.
- Your prediction should include whether or not you think the hypothesis is true, and an explanation. i.e. I think the hypothesis is true because…
- When answering questions about 'fair tests' it's always a good idea to explain why it is important to keep a particular variable the same, in terms of what might happen if it changed. For example, in an investigation about the effect of concentration on the rate of reaction, it's important to keep the temperature the same, because increasing temperature also increases the rate of reaction.

② A student carried out a reaction between limestone, $CaCO_3$, and hydrochloric acid, HCl. To find out the effect of changing the concentration of acid on the rate of reaction, the student used 4 different concentrations of hydrochloric acid and measured the carbon dioxide gas given off, and recorded the following results.

Time/s	Volume of carbon dioxide / c^3 for each concentration of HCl			
	0.5 mol/dm³	1 mol/dm³	1.5 mol/dm³	2 mol/dm³
30	0	0	0	0
60	5	10	15	20
90	10	20	30	40
120	15	30	45	60
150	20	40	60	80
180	25	50	70	85
210	30	60	80	90
240	35	65	85	95
270	40	70	90	97
300	45	80	92	98
330	47.5	85	95	99
360	50	88	97	99.5
390	51	90	95	100
420	52	92	99	100
450	53	94	100	100
480	54	95	100	100

a **Plot a graph of the results.** (5 marks, ★★★)

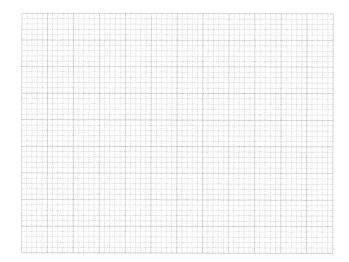

b **Use your graph to calculate the rate of reaction for each concentration of concentration of acid.** (4 marks, ★★★)

....

MATHS SKILLS

Remember that the independent variable (the one you change) goes on the x-axis on your graph. The dependent variable (the one you measure) goes on the y-axis.

Reversible reactions

① The decomposition of ammonium chloride is a reversible reaction:

ammonium chloride $\rightleftharpoons$ ammonia + hydrogen chloride

$$NH_4Cl(s) \rightleftharpoons NH_3(g) + HCl(g)$$

NAILIT!

Relatively few reactions are reversible – for example, most combustion reactions are generally irreversible!

a **What symbol tells you that the reaction is reversible?** (1 mark, ★)

....

b **Which of the following statements about reversible reactions is correct? Tick one box.** (1 mark, ★)

Reversible reactions can go both forwards and backwards in certain conditions.	
All reactions are reversible to some extent.	
Reversible reactions stop when they reach equilibrium.	
If the forward reaction is endothermic, the backward reaction must also be endothermic.	

NAILIT!

When a reversible reaction reaches a dynamic equilibrium the reaction does not stop. The forwards reaction is simply happening at the same rate as the backwards reaction. The concentration of reactants and products stays the same.

c **Explain what is meant by the term dynamic equilibrium.** (2 marks, ★★)

....

....

② A student heats limestone, $CaCO_3$, to produce lime, CaO, and carbon dioxide, as shown below:

$$CaCO_3 \rightleftharpoons CaO + CO_2$$

The reaction is reversible. The student collects the carbon dioxide in an upturned measuring cylinder in a trough of water.

NAILIT!

Remember that for reversible reactions if the forward reaction (Left to Right) is exothermic, the backward reaction (Right to Left) must be endothermic.

a **Explain what is meant by the term reversible reaction.** (2 marks, ★★)

....

b **Determine whether the backwards reaction is endothermic or exothermic. Explain your answer.** (3 marks, ★★★)

....

....

c **Explain why, after some time, the volume of carbon dioxide stops increasing and remains the same.** (3 marks, ★★★★)

....

....

(H) The effect of changing conditions on equilibrium

H(1) **Complete the sentence about dynamic equilibrium below.** (1 mark, ★)

At dynamic equilibrium, the rate of the forward reaction is ....

....

H(2) **Give three factors that can be changed that may change the position of equilibrium.** (3 marks, ★)

a ....

b ....

c ....

> **NAILIT!**
>
> If the temperature is increased the equilibrium will shift in favour of the reaction which is accompanied by a decrease in temperature. This means that if the backward reaction is endothermic then more reactants are formed.

H(3) **Define Le Chatelier's Principle.** (3 marks, ★★)

....

....

....

H(4) **In the Haber process, nitrogen and hydrogen produce ammonia, a valuable product which has many uses. The process is shown in the reaction shown below:**

~400°C
~200atm pressure
Iron catalyst
$N_2(g) + 3H_2(g) \rightleftharpoons 2NH_3(g)$ (+ heat)

> **NAILIT!**
>
> If you increase the concentration of one of the products then the system will try to lower its concentration by forming more reactants.

a **Describe what would happen if the temperature was increased.** (3 marks, ★★★)

....

....

b **Suggest a possible reason the reaction isn't carried out at room temperature.**
(1 mark, ★★★)

....

....

c **Explain the effect that the iron catalyst has on the reaction.**
(3 marks, ★★★)

....

....

> **NAILIT!**
>
> A catalyst has no effect on the position of equilibrium. It speeds up how quickly equilibrium is reached.

d **Explain why the Haber process is carried out at high pressure.**
(2 marks, ★★★★)

....

....

Organic chemistry

(1) **Explain each of the following facts about alkanes.**

    a **Alkanes are hydrocarbons.** (1 mark, ★)

    ....

    b **Alkanes are described as saturated.** (1 mark, ★★)

    ....

    c **Alkanes form a homologous series.** (2 marks, ★★★)

    ....

> **NAILIT!**
>
> The trends in the physical properties of alkanes are linked to the number of carbon atoms they have.
>
> As the number of carbon atoms increases, boiling points and viscosity increase, and flammability decreases.

(2) **State the formulae for the following alkanes.** (4 marks, ★★)

    a **Alkane with 20 carbon atoms.**   ....

    b **Alkane with 18 hydrogen atoms.**   ....

(3) **Complete the dot and cross diagram to show the bonding in ethane.** (2 marks, ★★)

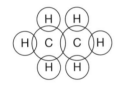

> **DOIT!**
>
> Remember the general formula for alkanes, C_nH_{2n+2}. You can then use this to predict the formula of any alkane if you are given the number of carbon or hydrogen atoms.

(4) **Heptane is an alkane which contains 7 carbon atoms.**

    a **Draw out its displayed formula.** (1 mark, ★★)

    b **State its molecular formula.** (1 mark, ★★) ....

(5) **Which of these alkanes is the most flammable? Tick one box.** (1 mark, ★★)

CH_4	
C_3H_8	

(7) **Which of these alkanes is the most viscous? Tick one box.** (1 mark, ★★)

C_2H_6	
C_4H_{10}	

(6) **Which of these alkanes has the highest boiling point? Tick one box.** (1 mark, ★★)

Propane	
Pentane	

Fractional distillation

(1) **Crude oil is separated into fractions by fractional distillation. Fractions are mixture of hydrocarbons which contain similar numbers of carbon atoms, and therefore have similar physical properties.**

Describe how fractional distillation separates crude oil into fractions. (4 marks, ★★★★)

NAILIT!

Note: use the key words **heat**, **evaporate**, **condense** and **boiling points** when describing fractional distillation.

....

....

(2) **Two of the fractions produced during fractional distillation are in the table below.**

Name of fraction	Use	Example of alkane in this fraction	Molecular formula of alkane	Boiling point of alkane/°C
Petroleum gases	Household fuels	Methane	CH_4	−162
Kerosene		Dodecane		214

Kerosene contains an alkane called dodecane, which has 12 carbon atoms.

a **State a use for kerosene.** (1 mark, ★★) ....

b **What is the molecular formula for dodecane?** (1 mark, ★★) ....

c **Explain why dodecane has a higher boiling point than methane.** (1 mark, ★★)

....

WORKIT!

Balance the equation to show the **complete combustion** of butane, C_4H_{10}.

$$C_4H_{10} + O_2 \rightarrow CO_2 + H_2O$$

Step 1 Balance the carbon atoms. There are 4 in butane, so this means 4 × CO_2

$$C_4H_{10} + O_2 \rightarrow 4CO_2 + H_2O$$

Step 2 Balance the hydrogen atoms. There are 10 in butane, which means 5 × H_2O

$$C_4H_{10} + O_2 \rightarrow 4CO_2 + 5H_2O$$

Step 3 Finally, balance the oxygen atoms. There are now 9 in total. Remember, you have O_2, so you need to halve 9. It's ok to use a fraction - half of 9 is 9/2 or 4½

$$C_4H_{10} + 9/2 O_2 \rightarrow 4CO_2 + 5H_2O$$

(3) **Write balanced symbol equations to show the complete combustion of:**

a **Ethane** (2 marks, ★★★) ....

b **Propane** (2 marks, ★★★) ....

c **Pentane** (2 marks, ★★★) ....

Cracking and alkenes

(1) **Explain why alkenes are described as unsaturated hydrocarbons.** (2 marks, ★★★)

....

....

NAILIT!

- Learn the products for the addition reactions for alkenes.
- Alkene + hydrogen → **alkane**
- Alkene + steam → **alcohol**
- Alkene + halogen → **dihaloalkane (an alkane with 2 halogens attached to it)**

(2) **Alkenes undergo addition reactions with hydrogen, steam and halogens.**

a **Write equations for these reactions, ensuring that the organic reactants and products are fully displayed.**

i **Pentene + hydrogen** (2 marks, ★★★) ....

ii **Butene + steam** (2 marks, ★★★) ....

iii **Propene + chlorine** (2 marks, ★★★) ....

b **Explain why the addition reactions of alkenes show 100% atom economy.** (1 mark, ★★)

....

(3) **Complete these equations to show the missing substances.** (5 marks, ★★★)

a $C_8H_{18} \rightarrow C_5H_{12} +$ ....
d $C_{14}H_{30} \rightarrow C_4H_{10} + C_6H_{12} +$ ....

b $C_{18}H_{38} \rightarrow C_3H_6 +$ ....
e $C_{14}H_{30} \rightarrow C_8H_{18} + 2$ ....

c .... $\rightarrow C_4H_8 + C_9H_{20}$

(4) **Decane is an alkane with 10 carbon atoms. Two possible products when it undergoes cracking are hexane, C_6H_{14}, and another compound, Z, which decolourises bromine water.**

a **What is the formula for decane?** (1 mark, ★) ....

b **Suggest a use for hexane.** (1 mark, ★★) ....

c **Why does compound Z decolourise bromine water?** (1 mark, ★★) ....

d **Suggest a use for compound Z.** (1 mark, ★★) ....

e **Work out the formula for compound Z and use this to construct the overall equation for the cracking of decane.** (1 mark, ★★★)

....

Alcohols

1 **Some alcohols are shown in the table below.**

CH$_3$CH$_2$CH$_2$OH	H—C—C—C—C—O—H (with H atoms above and below each C)
A	**B**
H—C—C—O—H (with H atoms)	CH$_3$OH
C	**D**

Which letter represents:

a **Butanol?** (1 mark, ★★) ....

b **Methanol?** (1 mark, ★★) ....

c **The alcohol with the molecular formula C$_3$H$_8$O?** (1 mark, ★★)

....

d **The alcohol formed when sugars are fermented?** (1 mark, ★★)

....

e **The alcohol with the highest boiling point?** (1 mark, ★★★) ....

2 **Alcohols make excellent fuels and when they burn in plenty of air, complete combustion takes place.**

Complete the word and symbol equations to show the complete combustion of the following alcohols. (4 marks, ★★★)

a **Methanol + oxygen →** .... + ...

.... **CH$_3$OH +** .... **O$_2$ →** .... + ...

b **Propanol + oxygen →** .... + ...

.... **CH$_3$CH$_2$CH$_2$OH +** .... **O$_2$ →** .... + ...

NAILIT!

Don't forget the extra 'O' in the alcohol when you are balancing combustion equations.

3 **Describe what would be seen in the following experiments.**

a **A small piece of sodium is added to butanol.** (2 marks, ★★★)

....

b **Ethanol is added to water.** (1 mark, ★★)

....

c **Propanol is mixed with acidified potassium dichromate.** (1 mark, ★★)

....

Carboxylic acids

(1) **Some organic substances with four carbon atoms are shown in the table below.**

C_4H_8	H H H O | | | // H—C—C—C—C | | | \\ H H H OH	$CH_3CH_2CH_2CH_2OH$
A	**B**	**C**
H O | // H—C—C H H | \\ | | H O—C—C—H | | H H	C_4H_{10}	
D	**E**	

Which letter represents:

a **Butane?** (1 mark, ★★) ....

b **A substance that will decolourise bromine water?** (1 mark, ★★) ....

c **Butanol?** (1 mark, ★★) ....

d **A substance that will produce carbon dioxide when added to sodium carbonate?**
(1 mark, ★★★) ....

e **A substance that is formed when a carboxylic acid and alcohol are heated with an acid catalyst?** (1 mark, ★★★) ....

f **The substance that can be oxidised to form butanoic acid?** (1 mark, ★★★★) ....

DO IT!

Carboxylic acids are **weak** acids. Review the topic about strong and weak acids to remind you about full and partial ionisation of acids in solution.

(2) **The general formula for carboxylic acids is $C_nH_{2n}O_2$.**

a **State the formula of the carboxylic acid with 8 carbon atoms.** (1 mark, ★★)

....

b **State the formula and the name of the carboxylic acid with 6 hydrogen atoms.** (2 marks, ★★)

....

(3) **The pH of 0.1 mol/dm³ hydrochloric acid is 1.00, whilst the pH of ethanoic acid of the same concentration is 2.88.**

Explain the difference in these pH values. You should use an equation in your answer.
(5 marks, ★★★★)

....

....

....

....

Addition polymerisation

1. The alkenes below undergo addition polymerisation to form polymers.

   For each monomer, draw out the repeating unit, and name the **polymer** formed. (8 marks, ★★★★)

Monomer	Repeating unit	Name of polymer
Ethene		
Chloroethene		
Ethenol		
Butene		

2. Draw out the displayed formulae for the monomers that would be used to make the polymers below. (2 marks, ★★★)

Repeating unit	Monomer

3. Pentene can undergo addition polymerisation to form a polymer.

   a The formula for pentene is C_5H_{10}. Write an equation, using displayed formulae, to show the formation of the polymer. (2 marks, ★★★★)

   ....

   b **Name the polymer formed.** (1 mark, ★) ....

Condensation polymerisation

H① **Five compounds are represented by the letters A, B, C, D and E.**

HO–CH$_2$–CH$_2$–OH	CH$_3$–CH$_2$–OH	H$_2$O	HOOC–CH$_2$–CH$_2$–CH$_2$–CH$_2$–COOH	CH$_3$–CH$_2$–COOH
A	**B**	**C**	**D**	**E**

a **Which two substances could be used to form a condensation polymer?** (2 marks, ★★★)

....

b **What other product would be formed when these two substances react together?**
(1 mark, ★★) ....

c **Name the functional group found in both A and B.** (1 mark, ★★) ....

d **Name the functional group found in both D and E.** (1 mark, ★★) ....

H② **The general equation to form a condensation polymer can be represented as follows:**

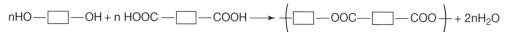

a **Write an equation like this for the reaction between ethanedioic acid and ethane diol. Their structures are shown below.** (3 marks, ★★★★★)

> **NAILIT!**
>
> For condensation polymerisation to occur there must be:
>
> - **2** different monomers
> - each monomer must have **2** functional groups.

HOOC–CH$_2$–CH$_2$–COOH	HO–CH$_2$–CH$_2$–OH
Ethanedioic acid	**Ethane diol**

....

b **Explain why the atom economy for producing condensation polymers is not 100%.**
(1 mark, ★★★)

....

....

c **Name the functional group formed during this type of polymerisation.** (1 mark, ★★)

....

....

H③ **Deduce the monomers used to form the condensation polymer below.** (2 marks, ★★★★★)

....

....

DOIT!

Learn the differences between addition and condensation polymerisation. Compare the atom economy, number of monomers, functional groups and number of products.

Amino acids and DNA

(1) **Choose the words from the box to complete the sentences below.** (4 marks, ★★)

Two amino acids can join together by .... polymerisation to form polypeptides

and ....

Each amino acid contains two functional groups, a .... acid group which has the

formula –COOH and an amine group, which has the formula –NH$_2$. The –COOH on one

amino acid reacts with the –NH$_2$ group on another amino acid forming a polymer, with the

elimination of ....

carboxylic hydrogen addition strong water condensation weak proteins starch

(2) **The simplest amino acid is called *glycine*, and has the formula H$_2$NCH$_2$COOH. When it undergoes polymerisation it forms the polypeptide shown in the equation below.**

n H$_2$NCH$_2$COOH → (–HNCH$_2$COO–)$_n$ + nH$_2$O

Another amino acid *alanine*, has the formula H$_2$NCH(CH$_3$)COOH

Different amino acids can be combined to form proteins. The amino acids are linked by the peptide bond:

–NHCO–

a **Write out an equation to show the polymerisation of alanine.** (2 marks, ★★★★)

....

....

b **Write out an equation to show how glycine and alanine can combine together to form a polymer.** (3 marks, ★★★★★)

....

....

(3) **DNA is a naturally occurring polymer which is essential for life. State the name of the monomers used to form DNA.** (1 mark, ★★)

....

(4) **Starch and glucose are both polysaccharides. What type of monomers are used to form polysaccharides?** (1 mark, ★★)

....

DO IT!

Create a table of naturally occurring polymers and the names of the types of polymers which they are made from.

Chemical analysis

Pure substances and formulations

(1) **Explain what is meant by the term pure.** (1 mark, ★)

....

(2) **Milk is sometimes described as pure.**

> **NAILIT!**
>
> Pure substances have specific melting and boiling points, mixtures melt and boil over a range of temperatures.

a **Explain why describing milk as pure is misleading.**
(2 marks, ★★)

....

b **Explain how you could show this in an experiment.** (3 marks, ★★★)

....

....

(3) **Pure aspirin melts at 136°C. A sample of an aspirin tablet starts to melt at 125°C. What does this tell you about the aspirin tablet?** (1 mark, ★★★)

....

....

> **NAILIT!**
>
> Sometimes it is necessary to use more than one technique to test the identity and purity of a substance. Work through the following pages – what could you do to confirm that the pure water from distillation contains no sodium chloride salt?

(4) **One way to make pure water is from salt water, using a process known as distillation, shown in the diagram below.**

Heat

a **Label the diagram to show (i) salt water, (ii) pure water vapour (iii) pure water.**
(3 marks, ★★)

b **Explain how distillation allows pure water to be produced from salt water.** (3 marks, ★★★)

....

....

(5) A paracetamol tablet has a mass of 2 g. It contains 500 mg of paracetamol, $C_8H_9NO_2$, 1.25 g of starch, $C_6H_{10}O_5$, a bulking agent, and 0.25 g of magnesium stearate, $Mg(C_{18}H_{35}O_2)_2$, a lubricant to prevent the tablet sticking to the packaging.

a Explain why the paracetamol tablet is an example of a formulation. (1 mark, ★)

....

b Calculate the percentage composition of paracetamol in the tablet, in terms of mass.
(2 marks, ★★★)

....

....

H c Calculate the number of moles of each compound in the tablet. (6 marks, ★★★★)

   i Paracetamol

....

....

   ii Starch

....

....

   iii Magnesium stearate.

....

....

d Calculate the percentage composition of paracetamol in the tablet, in terms of moles.
(2 marks, ★★★★)

MATHSSKILLS

The formulae you will need for formulation calculations are:

$$\text{Percentage} = \frac{\text{mass of component}}{\text{total mass}} \times 100\%$$

$$\text{Number of moles} = \frac{\text{mass}}{\text{Mr}}$$

....

....

....

....

....

Chromatography

(1) **Tick two statements that are correct.** (2 marks, ★)

Chromatography is a technique that can be used to separate mixtures into their components.	
Chromatography works because different compounds have different levels of attraction for the paper and the solvent.	
Chromatography involves three phases – a mobile phase, a stationary phase and a dynamic phase.	
Chromatography is a technique that can be used to create mixtures from their components.	
Chromatography gives you information about the quantity of the components in a mixture.	

NAILIT!

Remember that water isn't the only solvent that can be used for the mobile phase. Often, scientists will try different solvents until there is a good separation between the spots. Commonly used solvents include: ethanol, dichloromethane and ethyl ethanoate.

(2) **A student wanted to identify the inks used in a black pen. He set up the equipment as shown below.**

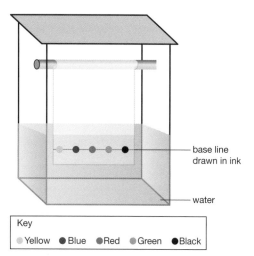

base line drawn in ink

water

Key
● Yellow ● Blue ● Red ● Green ● Black

a **Suggest two errors in the way the student has set up the experiment. Explain the problems each of these errors would cause.** (4 marks, ★★)

....

....

....

....

....

b **The R_f value for the yellow ink is 0.88. The R_f value for the green ink is 0.84. Dot C has travelled 22 cm. Calculate the R_f of dot C and identify its colour.** (3 marks, ★★★)

....

....

MATHSKILLS

In the exam, you may need to rearrange the formula:

R_f = Distance moved by spot/distance moved by solvent

Distance moved by the spot = R_f × distance moved by the solvent

Distance moved by the solvent = R_f × distance moved by the spot

Testing for gases

(1) **Match the gas to its test and result if it is present. Chlorine has been done for you.** (3 marks, ★)

Hydrogen	a glowing splint put into a test tube of the gas	is extinguished with a 'pop'
Oxygen	bubble the gas through a solution of limewater	produces solid calcium carbonate, turning the limewater cloudy
Carbon dioxide	expose to litmus or UI paper	bleaches the paper
Chlorine	a lighted splint put into a test tube of the gas	relights

(2) **For each of the following, identify the gas being tested.** (4 marks, ★★)

a **The gas turns limewater turns cloudy.** ....

b **The gas bleaches litmus paper.** ....

c **The gas extinguishes a lighted splint with a pop.** ....

d **The gas relights a glowing splint.** ....

(3) **For the following reactions, describe the test that could be used to confirm the gases produced.** (4 marks, ★★)

a $CH_4 + 2O_2 \rightarrow CO_2 + 2H_2O$ ....

b $Mg + H_2SO_4 \rightarrow MgSO_4 + H_2$ ....

c $CO_2 + H_2O \rightarrow C_6H_{12}O_6 + O_2$ ....

d $HCl + MnO_2 \rightarrow MnCl_2 + 2H_2O + Cl_2$ ....

(4) **A student sets up an experiment using limewater to test the gases produced by a lit candle.**

Explain what the student will observe, and how they could find out whether the candle produces other gases. (6 marks, ★★★).

NAILIT!

Chlorine gas is toxic – reactions involving the production of it should be done in small quantities and in a fume cupboard.

NAILIT!

Hydrogen is actually a very flammable gas and can cause explosions. The pop you hear is actually a tiny explosion!

SNAPIT!

You are expected to remember each of the tests for gases.

- Carbon dioxide – limewater
- Oxygen – relight
- Hydrogen – pop
- Chlorine - bleach

....
....
....
....
....
....
....

Identifying metal ions using flame tests, flame emission spectroscopy and sodium hydroxide

(1) **Match the metal salt to the colour of the flame when heated on a Bunsen burner.** (5 marks, ★)

Lithium carbonate	Lilac
Sodium chloride	Crimson
Potassium sulfate	Orange-red
Calcium nitrate	Green
Copper phosphate	Yellow

(2) **A flame emission spectroscope was used to identify a mixture of metal salts. Four known ions were analysed, followed by the unknown sample, Y.**

Lithium
Potassium
Sodium
Copper
Y

a **Identify the two ions in Y.** (2 marks, ★★)

....

....

....

b **To calibrate the spectroscope, a student ran solutions of pure lithium of increasing concentration and recorded the line intensity in the table below.**

Conc.mg/cm³	0.00	0.10	0.20	0.40	0.80	1.00
Line intensity	0.000	0.013	0.026	0.055	0.110	0.124

i **Plot a graph of the data.** (2 marks, ★★)

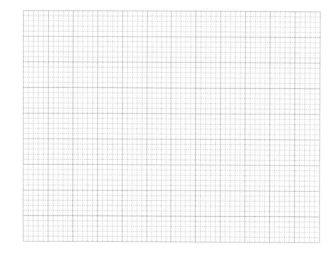

MATHSKILLS

Concentration goes on the x-axis of calibration graphs.

To find an unknown, use a ruler find the intersect of a curve or line of best fit.

ii **Use your graph to determine the concentration of a sample which gives a line intensity of 0.041.** (1 mark, ★★★)

....

iii **Use your graph to predict the line intensity of a sample which contains 0.6 mg/cm³ of lithium.** (1 mark, ★★★)

....

Testing for negative ions (anions) in salts

(1) **Match the negative ion with the procedure to test for it and what would happen in a positive test.** (5 marks, ★)

Chloride (Cl⁻)	Hydrochloric acid then pass gas formed through limewater	White precipitate (of silver chloride)
Bromide (Br⁻)	Hydrochloric acid followed by barium chloride solution	Cream precipitate (of silver bromide)
Iodide (I⁻)	Nitric acid followed by silver nitrate solution	Yellow precipitate (of silver iodide)
Sulfate (SO_4^{2-})	Nitric acid followed by silver nitrate solution	White precipitate (of barium sulfate)
Carbonate (CO_3^{2-})	Nitric acid followed by silver nitrate solution	Effervescence and gas turns limewater cloudy/milky

(2) **A student wanted to find out what other substances are added to table salt, NaCl.**

The student conducted an investigation and recorded the results as shown below.

Test	Description	Observations
1	Dilute nitric acid was added to the table salt and the gas passed through limewater	The mixture effervesced and the gas turned limewater cloudy
2	Nitric acid was added to the salt, and then silver nitrate solution was added	A white precipitate formed

a **What does this tell you about the negative ions in the table salt?** (2 marks, ★★)

....

....

b **Explain why the student used nitric acid in test 1 rather than hydrochloric acid.** (2 marks, ★★★)

....

....

c **Identify the white precipitate that formed in test 2.** (1 mark, ★★★) ....

H d **Write a balanced equation for the reaction that takes place in test 1.** (1 mark, ★★★)

....

NAILIT!

If you are asked to write the symbol equations for the reactions of halides and sulfate you must remember that the negative ion combines with the metal in the test reagent to form a solid. So for potassium bromide:

Ionic equation: Full equation:

$Ag^+(aq) + Br^-(aq) \rightarrow AgBr(s)$ $AgNO_3(aq) + KBr(aq) \rightarrow KNO_3(aq) + AgBr(s)$

Identifying ions in an ionic compound

(1) **A compound contains either calcium or lithium ions, and either chloride or bromide ions.**

    a **Suggest how you would identify which of the positive ions the compound contains. You must include what colours you could expect to find in your answer.** (1 mark, ★)

    ....

    b **Suggest how you would identify which of the negative ions the compound contains. You must include what colours you could expect to find in your answer.** (1 mark, ★)

    ....

(2) **Explain how you would identify the ions in sodium sulfate.** (4 marks, ★★)

....

....

(3) **A student carries out a series of experiments to identify four unknown compounds, as shown in the table below.**

Substance	Flame test	Sodium hydroxide	Barium chloride solution	Silver nitrate solution	Hydrochloric acid
A	Lilac	No reaction	No reaction	No reaction	Effervescence and gas turned limewater milky
B	Red	White precipitate	White precipitate	No reaction	No reaction
C	No colour	White precipitate, dissolves in excess	No reaction	Cream precipitate	No reaction
D	Orange-brown	Brown precipitate	No reaction	Yellow precipitate	No reaction

Identify substances A to D. (4 marks, ★★★)

A ....   B ....

C ....   D ....

(4) **A student reacts hydrochloric acid with calcium carbonate, producing water, carbon dioxide and a salt.**
Explain how you would identify the ions in the salt and what you would expect to find.
(4 marks, ★★★)

....

....

NAILIT!

In the exam, you may be asked about colour changes you don't recognise. Where that happens, focus on the colour changes you do recognise as they may provide a clue.

NAILIT!

Check back through your notes for this topic to answer these questions.

The composition and evolution of the Earth's atmosphere

1 a Tick **two** processes that reduced the amount of carbon dioxide in the atmosphere. (2 marks, ★)

Carbonate rock formation	
Respiration by animals	
Fossil fuel combustion	
Fossil fuel formation	

b What reduced the amount of water vapour in the atmosphere? (1 mark, ★★)

....

....

....

c Explain how this affected the amount of carbon dioxide in the atmosphere? (2 marks, ★★)

....

d Photosynthesis by algae, bacteria and later, plants, is thought to have significantly reduced the amount of carbon dioxide in the atmosphere. Write the balanced symbol equation for the reaction. (2 marks, ★★)

....

2 Some students set up an experiment to investigate what percentage of air is oxygen, as shown in the diagram below.

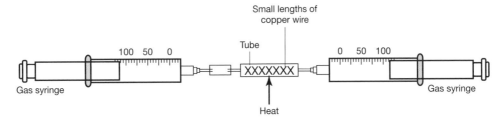

100 cm³ of air is drawn into the syringe. When heated, the oxygen in the air reacts with the copper in the tube. At the end of the experiment, the volume of gas in the syringe had reduced to 78.5 cm³. The equation for the reaction is:

.........$Cu + O_2 \rightarrow$ ....CuO

a Balance the equation. (1 mark, ★)

b Calculate the percentage of oxygen in the 100 cm³ of sample air. (1 mark, ★★)

....

c Explain why it is important to allow the apparatus to cool before recording the result. (2 marks, ★★)

....

....

Global warming

(1) It is known that some gases are greenhouse gases that have the potential to increase global temperatures. It is also known that human activity has increased the amount of some of these greenhouse gases in the atmosphere. To understand the possible consequences, scientists have created climate models that they use to try to predict future changes to the Earth's climate.

a Give **one** reason why it is difficult to create models to predict future climate change. (1 mark, ★)

....

b Describe what is meant by the term **peer review.** (1 mark, ★★)

....

c Identify **two** greenhouse gases. (2 marks, ★)

....

d Describe how human activity has increased the amount of these two gases in the atmosphere. (4 marks, ★★)

....

....

(2) The graph below shows how temperatures and the amount of CO_2 have changed over the last 400 000 years.

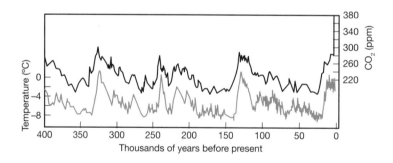

a Suggest **two** conclusions you could make from the data in the graph. (2 marks, ★★★)

....

....

b One theory about climate change is that temperatures on Earth have always changed with natural increases and decreases in the amount of CO_2 in the atmosphere and that the current situation is no different. Use the data in the graph and your knowledge to **evaluate** this theory. (4 marks, ★★★★)

....

....

....

....

The carbon footprint and its reduction

(1) **Match the method of reducing the carbon footprint to the description of how it works.**
(3 marks, ★★)

Alternative energy	Removing the carbon dioxide given out by power stations by reacting it with other chemicals. The product of this reaction can then be stored deep under the sea in porous sedimentary rocks.
Energy conservation	Plants take in carbon dioxide as they grow, when they are burned they only release the same amount of carbon dioxide. This makes them carbon neutral.
Carbon Capture and Storage (CCS)	Renewable energy sources such as solar cells, wind power and wave power do not rely on the burning of fossil fuels.
Carbon taxes	Reducing the amount of energy used by using energy-saving measures such as house insulation, using devices that use less energy, reduces the demand for energy.
	Penalising companies and individuals who use too much energy by increasing their taxes reduces the demand for energy.
Carbon offsetting	
Using plants as biofuels	Removing carbon dioxide from the air using natural biological processes such as photosynthesis. This is achieved by planting trees and increasing marine algae by adding chemicals to the oceans.

(2) The table shows the annual carbon footprint (in tonnes per person) of some countries in 1990 and 2011.

Country	Carbon footprint (tonnes/person) 1990	Carbon footprint (tonnes/person) 2011
Qatar	25.2	44.0
USA	19.1	17
UK	10	7.1
Greece	7.2	7.6
New Zealand	7.1	7.1
China	2.2	7.2
India	0.7	1.2

a **Suggest two reasons that countries such as the USA and Qatar have carbon footprints much higher than China or India.** (2 marks, ★★)

....

....

b **Describe how the carbon footprint in the UK has changed since 1990.**
(1 mark, ★)

....

c **Explain why some countries have seen an increase in their carbon footprints since 1990.** (3 marks, ★★★)

....

....

....

Atmospheric pollutants

① **Match the pollutant with its effects and ways to reduce its release in the atmosphere.**
(4 marks, ★★)

Soot		
	Dissolves in clouds to cause acid rain and causes respiratory problems	Ensure complete combustion of fossil fuels
Carbon monoxide	A toxic gas which binds to haemoglobin in the blood, preventing the transport of oxygen around the body	Desulfurisation of petrochemicals before combustion
Sulfur dioxide	Global dimming and lung damage	Ensure complete combustion of fossil fuels
Oxides of nitrogen	Dissolves in clouds to cause acid rain and causes respiratory problems	Catalytic converters used after combustion

② **The table below shows information about the pollutants emitted by cars which use diesel and petrol fuels.**

Fuel	Relative amount of CO_2	Relative amount of SO_2	Relative amount of particulate matter	Relative amount of oxides of nitrogen
Diesel	80	40	100	30
Petrol	100	10	0	20

a **Compare the pollutants from cars using petrol as their fuel to those using diesel.** (3 marks, ★★)

....

....

....

b **Electric cars emit no pollutants directly and are powered by batteries that are recharged by plugging them into an electrical plug socket. Suggest how powering these vehicles may still release pollutants into the atmosphere.** (2 marks, ★★)

....

....

H③ **The use of coal to produce electricity has in recent decades reduced in many countries. However, with reducing oil supplies, some countries are considering building new coal power stations. The chemical reaction for the complete combustion of coal is:**

$4C_{240}H_{90}O_4NS + 1053O_2 \rightarrow 960CO_2 + 174H_2O + 4HNO_3 + 4H_2SO_4$

a **Calculate the number of moles of carbon dioxide released when 8 moles of coal is burned in an excess of oxygen.** (2 marks, ★★)

....

b **In the 1950s, thousands of people in London died during the 'London Smog'. Many of these deaths were due to high levels of sulfur dioxide in the atmosphere released by the burning of fossil fuels such as coal. Using the balanced equation above, explain how burning coal can also cause damage to limestone buildings, trees and plant crops.** (2 marks, ★★★)

....

....

Finite and renewable resources, sustainable development

1 **Fill the gaps to complete the sentence about finite and renewable resources.** (5 marks, ★)

The .... used by chemists to make new materials can be divided into two categories –

.... and .... resources will run out. Examples are fossil fuels and

various metals. .... resources are ones that can be replaced at the same rate as they

are used up. They are derived from plant materials.

.... meets the needs of present development without depleting natural resources for

future generations.

| natural resources | finite | renewable | sustainable development |

(some words are used twice)

2 **State four characteristics of a sustainable process.** (4 marks, ★)

....

....

....

....

> **NAILIT!**
>
> Look over your notes on atom economy and percentage yield as you may be asked to compare the sustainability of reactions in terms of quantitatively using them.

3 **Explain how the use of catalysts helps make chemical reactions more sustainable.** (2 marks, ★★)

....

....

4 **Two companies produce a plastic used to manufacture goods. Company A uses a method where they expect to produce 25 kg. Company B uses a method where they expect to produce 19 kg. Company A actually produces 22 kg and Company B actually produces 18 kg.**

a **Calculate the percentage yield for both companies.** (2 marks, ★★)

....

....

....

b **Suggest which company uses the more sustainable method.** (1 mark, ★★)

....

....

....

....

> **NAILIT!**
>
> Sustainable processes:
>
> - have reactions with high atom economy with as few waste products as possible;
> - use renewable resources from plant sources;
> - have as few steps as possible to eliminate waste and increase the yield;
> - use catalysts to save energy.

Life cycle assessments (LCAs)

(1) **Explain what is meant by the term life cycle assessment.** (2 marks, ★)

....

....

(2) **List the stages of a life cycle assessment.** (2 marks, ★)

....

....

(3) a **Complete the table of the life cycle assessments of paper and plastic shopping bags.**
(4 marks, ★★)

Stage of LCA	Plastic bag	Paper bag
Source of raw materials		Come from trees
Production	Simple process involving no chemical change	
Use	Reusable	
End of life	Decompose slowly but produce less	Decompose quickly but generate more ....

b **Use the information in the table to compare the life cycle assessments of the paper and plastic shopping bags.** (2 marks, ★★★)

....

....

....

(4) **A supermarket that supplies its customers with plastic carrier bags ran the following advert:**

"Our carrier bags are environmentally friendly as their manufacture produces no harmful pollutants. They're also reusable."

Explain why the advert is misleading. (2 marks, ★★★)

....

....

....

Alternative methods of copper extraction

H 1 a **Complete the flow chart below to show how copper ores that are rich in copper can be extracted.** (1 mark, ★★)

copper rich ores → [ ] ┄┄┄ → [ ] → copper

  b **Suggest a reason why the copper produced by smelting may need to undergo electrolysis.** (1 mark, ★★)

  ....

H 2 **Tick two potential problems when using these processes.** (2 marks, ★)

Smelting and electrolysis use a lot of energy	
Copper-rich ores are scarce	
Copper is less reactive than iron	
Copper is used in many products	
Electrolysis is not necessary	

NAILIT!

Copper is a widely used metal – it is in coins, electrical wiring and motors, because it conducts heat and electricity well.

NAILIT!

Because copper is so widely used, copper-rich ores are scarce. Using traditional methods for ores that are low in copper is uneconomical – it costs more than the value of the copper produced. Developing alternative processes is an active area of research.

H 3 a **Tick three alternative methods that can be used to extract copper from low-grade ores.** (3 marks, ★)

Distillation using heat	
Bioleaching using bacteria	
Phytomining using plants	
Displacement using silver	
Displacement using iron	

NAILIT!

This is another topic where it's useful to know the order of reactivity of metals!

  b **Identify one advantage and one disadvantage for each of these methods.** (3 marks, ★★)

  i Advantage: .... Disadvantage: ....

  ii Advantage: .... Disadvantage: ....

  iii Advantage: .... Disadvantage: ....

Making potable water and waste water treatment

① **State what is meant by the term potable water.** (1 mark, ★)

....

② **Explain why potable water can't be described as 'pure water'.** (2 marks, ★)

....

③ **The flow chart below shows the different stages in the production of potable water.**

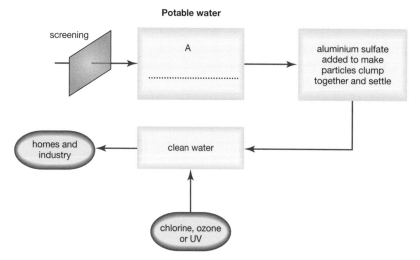

a **Fill in the gap in the box marked 'A' to identify what happens at that stage of potable water production.**

(1 mark, ★)

b **Suggest why chlorine, ozone or UV is used in this process.** (1 mark, ★★)

....

....

④ **One way to obtain potable water from salt water is by distillation.**

a **Identify one other way to obtain potable water from salt water.** (1 mark, ★)

....

b **Explain why distillation requires energy to heat the salt water.** (2 marks, ★★)

....

....

⑤ **The flow chart below shows how waste water is treated.**

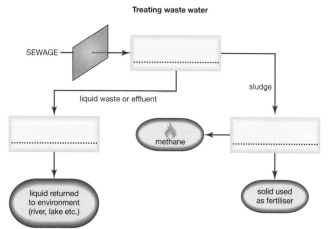

a **Complete the diagram to identify the stages of waste water treatment.** (4 marks, ★★)

b **Suggest what additional treatment may be needed for industrial waste before it can be released into the environment.** (1 mark, ★★★)

....

....

Ways of reducing the use of resources

(1) There are many benefits to reusing and recycling materials like glass, plastic and metal.

a Tick **two** statements which are not benefits of reusing glass bottles. (2 marks, ★)

Reduces use of limited raw materials to make glass bottles	
Reduces use of glass bottles	
Reduces demand for energy from limited resources	
Melting glass bottles to form new products requires energy	
Reduces use of limited raw materials to make other glass products	

NAILIT!

Remember that steel is an alloy of iron with specific amounts of carbon and other metals.

b Tick **three** statements which are processes involved in recycling metals. (3 marks, ★)

Separation	
Distillation	
Reforming	
Demineralisation	
Melting	
Cracking	

NAILIT!

Extracting metals from their ores is energy intensive. Look back at the metals topic to see how metals are extracted and how the reactivity of a metal impacts the amount of energy required to extract it.

(2) The table below shows data about the extraction and recycling of iron and aluminium.

	Iron		Aluminium	
	Extraction	Recycling	Extraction	Recycling
Relative energy use	70	30	95	5
Relative CO$_2$ emissions	70	30	95	5
Relative impact on ore deposits	100	0	100	0
Comments	Magnetic		Reactive	

a Suggest why iron is easy to separate from other metals. (1 mark, ★)

....

b Describe how recycled iron can reduce the amount of raw materials required to produce steel. (2 marks, ★★)

....

....

c Explain why increasing the amount of aluminium that is recycled is important. (3 marks, ★★★)

....

....

Rusting

(1) **Define the term corrosion.** (1 mark, ★)

....

(2) **A student ran an experiment to investigate the effectiveness of different methods to prevent rust. The student recorded the mass of five nails and put them in different test tubes as shown below. The student left them for 14 days and then recorded the mass again.**

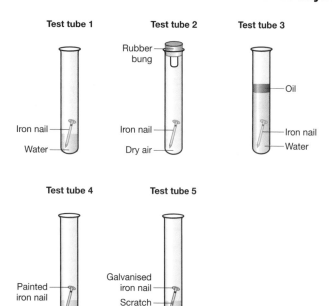

a Predict which nail will show the biggest increase in mass. (1 mark, ★★)

....

b Explain your answer. (3 marks, ★★★)

....

....

....

....

....

....

c **Rust is hydrated iron(III) oxide. Write the word equation for the reaction.**

.... + ... + ... → ....

The results of the experiment are shown in the table below.

Test tube	Mass before (g)	Mass after 14 days (g)
1	7.02	7.74
2	7.04	7.04
3	6.99	6.99
4	7.86	7.86
5	8.17	8.17

d **Explain why the mass of the nails in test tubes 2 to 5 did not increase.** (4 marks, ★★★)

Test tube 2: ....

Test tube 3: ....

Test tube 4: ....

Test tube 5: ....

e **Suggest a metal that could have been used to galvanise the nail in test tube 5. Explain your answer.** (3 marks, ★★★)

....

Alloys as useful materials

(1) **Circle the correct words to complete the sentence below.** (1 mark, ★)

	mixture		non-metals.
An alloy is a	compound	of	compounds.
	solution		metals.

(2) **Most pure metals are soft. They can be made harder by creating alloys.**

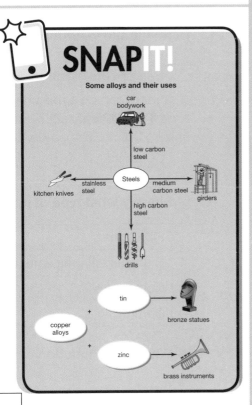

SNAPIT!

Some alloys and their uses

- car bodywork
- low carbon steel
- Steels
- stainless steel — kitchen knives
- medium carbon steel — girders
- high carbon steel
- drills
- tin — bronze statues
- copper alloys +
- zinc — brass instruments

   a **Suggest why the gold medals given at sporting events are usually made with an alloy containing gold, rather than pure gold.** (2 marks, ★★)

....

....

   b **Tick two statements that explain why pure gold is soft.** (2 marks, ★★★)

Gold ions are joined by strong ionic bonds	
Gold ions are arranged in layers	
Gold ions can slide over each other	
Gold ions are joined by strong covalent bonds	

   c **Explain how adding copper to gold makes it harder.** (2 marks, ★★★)

....

(3) **A company that manufactures steel is testing samples of the steel they have produced so that it can be sent to the companies that use it. The results of the tests are shown in the table below.**

	Steel sample A	Steel sample B	Steel sample C
Mass of iron (g)	25.40	24.80	25.10
Mass of carbon (g)	0.45	0.21	0.03

   a **Explain why a car bodywork manufacturer uses mild steel.** (2 marks, ★★★)

....

....

   b **Suggest which sample of steel would be most suitable for a bodywork manufacturer. Explain your answer.** (2 marks, ★★★)

....

....

   H c **Calculate the number of moles and percentage composition of iron and carbon in steel sample B.** (2 marks, ★★★★)

....

....

Ceramics, polymers and composites

(1) a **Match the material to its properties and components.** (1 mark, ★)

| Borosilicate glass | Strong and light | Metal ions and covalent structures |

| Fibre glass | High melting point | Strands of glass fibre and plastic resin |

| Ceramics | Hard, brittle, electrical insulators, waterproof | Silicon dioxide and boron trioxide |

b **Identify what type of material house bricks are made of. Tick one box.** (1 mark, ★)

Fibre glass	
High-density polyethene	
Composite	
Ceramic	

c **What is the function of the glass fibres and plastic resin in fibre glass?** (2 marks, ★★)

....

d **What is fibre glass an example of?** (1 mark, ★) ....

e **Explain why fibre glass is used to make cycling equipment.** (2 marks, ★★)

....

(2) **The diagrams below show four different polymers.**

i   ii   iii   iv

strong bond

a **Identify each polymer.**

i .... ii ....

iii .... iv ....

b **Explain the differences and similarities between HDPE and LDPE.** (4 marks, ★★)

....

....

....

c **Explain why milk bottles are easily recycled but plastic electrical components are more difficult to recycle.** (4 marks, ★★★)

....

....

....

The Haber process

(1) What is the product of the Haber process? Tick one box. (1 mark, ★)

Ammonia	
Nitrogen	
Nitrates	
Nitrites	

(2) Write a balanced symbol equation for the reaction. (2 marks, ★)

....

....

(3) Which of these describes the Haber process best? Tick one box. (1 mark, ★★)

The reaction is reversible and the forward reaction is exothermic. This means that the backward reaction is endothermic.	
The reaction is reversible and the forward reaction is endothermic. This means that the backward reaction is exothermic.	
The reaction is not reversible and the reaction is endothermic.	
The reaction is not reversible and the reaction is exothermic.	

(4) Describe the conditions of the Haber process. (3 marks, ★★)

....

....

H(5) Explain the conditions of the Haber process. (6 marks, ★★★)

....

....

....

H(6) The graph below shows the percentage yield of ammonia changes with pressure at different temperatures.

a Explain why the percentage yield of ammonia is higher at higher pressure. (2 marks, ★★)

....

....

b Explain why 350°C is described as a 'compromise'. (2 marks, ★★)

....

....

c Determine the percentage yield of ammonia at:

i   300 atmospheres and 400°C ....

ii   200 atmospheres and 350°C. ....

Production and uses of NPK fertilisers

(1) Using the words in the box below, fill the gaps to complete the sentence about fertilisers. (3 marks, ★)

Plants need compounds of ...., ... and .... for the growth and carrying out photosynthesis. .... containing these three elements are called ....

| nitrogen (N) | phosphorous (P) | potassium (K) | fertilisers | NPK fertilisers |

(2) Match the component compound of fertilizer to its source. (3 marks, ★★)

Ammonium nitrate, NH_4NO_3

Obtained by mining.

Ammonium hydrogen phosphate, $(NH_4)_2HPO_4$

Ammonia from the Haber process is oxidised to form nitric acid, which is then reacted with ammonia.

Mined phosphate rock is reacted with nitric acid to form phosphoric acid, H_3PO_4, which is reacted with ammonia.

Potassium chloride, KCl

(3) Fertilisers used by farmers usually has a label similar to the one below.

NPK 12:9:11

Explain why this information is useful to farmers. (2 marks, ★★)

....

....

(4) Complete the table below:

Fertiliser	Acid	Alkali
Ammonium nitrate		ammonia
Ammonium phosphate		ammonia
Ammonium sulfate		ammonia
Potassium nitrate		potassium hydroxide

(5) Calculate the percentage of phosphorous in ammonium hydrogen phosphate, $(NH_4)_2HPO_4$.
(2 marks, ★★★)

....

....

H (6) Calculate the number of moles of nitrogen in 500 g of ammonium nitrate, NH_4NO_3.
(3 marks, ★★★)

....

....

1.1 **The three states of matter can be represented by the simple particle model.**

a **Match each diagram to the correct state of matter.** (3 marks)

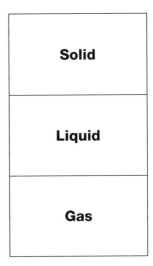
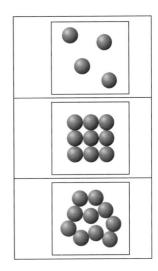

The temperature at which a substance changes from a liquid to a solid is known as the **freezing point**. This can be investigated by heating a solid until it melts and then recording the temperature at regular intervals as it cools.

Some results of an experiment are shown below.

Time/minutes	Temperature/°C
0	80
1	76
2	73
3	72
4	72
5	72
6	72
7	71
8	68
9	64
10	60

b **Choosing a suitable scale, plot these points on a piece of graph paper.** (3 marks)

c **Join up the points with a line and state the freezing point of this solid.** (2 marks)

H d **State one limitation of the simple particle model when it is used to explain changes of state.** (1 mark)

1.2 **Lithium reacts with chlorine to form lithium chloride.**

a **What is the correct formula for lithium chloride? Tick one box.** (1 mark)

Li_2Cl	
$LiCl_2$	
$LiCl$	
Li_2Cl_2	

b **Lithium also reacts with water to form an alkaline solution.**

Identify the ion responsible for making the solution alkaline. Tick one box.
(1 mark)

OH^+	
H^+	
H^-	
OH^-	

c **The formula for lithium oxide is Li_2O.**

What is its relative formula mass? Tick one box. (1mark)

14	
30	
22	
39	

1.3 **Lithium exists as two stable isotopes, ^6_3Li and ^7_3Li.**

Complete the table below to show the number of sub-atomic particles in each isotope. (3 marks)

Isotope	Number of protons	Number of electrons	Number of neutrons
^6_3Li			
^7_3Li			

1.4 **The most abundant isotope of lithium is ^7_3Li, which accounts for 92.5% of naturally occurring lithium.**

a **Calculate the percentage abundance of the ^6_3Li isotope.** (1 mark)

....

b **Use the information to work out the relative atomic mass of lithium to 1 decimal place.** (3 marks)

....

....

2.1 The table below shows some of the properties of calcium, chlorine and calcium chloride.

Substance	Formula	Type of bonding	Melting point	Electrical conductivity
Calcium	Ca		842	Good
Chlorine	Cl_2		−102	Does not conduct
Calcium chloride	$CaCl_2$		772	Conducts only when molten or in solution

a **Complete the table to show the type of bonding in these substances.** (3 marks)

....

....

b **Explain why calcium can conduct electricity.** (2 marks)

....

....

c **Complete the dot and cross diagram to show the bonding in a molecule of chlorine.**
(2 marks)

d **Use your ideas about structure and bonding to explain the melting points of calcium, chlorine and calcium chloride.** (6 marks)

....

....

....

....

....

2.2 Sodium is also in group 1.

    a Complete the diagram of the sodium atom. (1 mark)

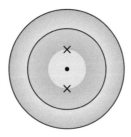

    b Explain why an atom of sodium is neutral. (1 mark)

....

2.3 In a reaction, 5 g of sodium reacts with an excess of oxygen to form sodium oxide.

    The equation for this reaction is as follows:

$$4Na(s) + O_2(g) \rightarrow 2Na_2O(s)$$

    a Explain what happens, in terms of electrons, when sodium reacts with oxygen. You can include diagrams in your answer. (4 marks)

....

....

....

    b Sodium oxide does not conduct electricity when solid, but will when molten or in solution. Explain why. (3 marks)

....

....

....

    H c Calculate the maximum mass of sodium oxide that could be formed in this reaction. (4 marks)

    [Na = 23, O = 16]

....

....

....

....

3.1 **Soluble salts can be formed by reacting dilute acids with bases. These are neutralisation reactions.**

a **Which of the following does not act as a base? Tick one box.**
(1 mark)

Calcium carbonate	
Lithium sulfate	
Potassium oxide	
Ammonia	

b **What is the pH of a neutral solution? Tick one box.**
(1 mark)

7	
14	
1	
3	

c **Which of the following is a weak acid? Tick one box.** (1 mark)

Sulfuric acid	
Ethanoic acid	
Nitric acid	
Hydrochloric acid	

3.2 **A student carries out an experiment to make magnesium chloride by reacting magnesium carbonate with hydrochloric acid. Carbon dioxide and water are also produced in the reaction.**

The equation for this reaction is: $MgCO_3(s) + 2HCl(aq) \rightarrow MgCl_2(aq) + CO_2(g) + H_2O(l)$

a **What is meant by the symbol (aq)?** (1 mark) ....

During this experiment, an excess of magnesium carbonate is added to $20\,cm^3$ of 2 mol/dm^3 hydrochloric acid. The excess magnesium carbonate is removed by filtration, and the resulting solution is heated over a water bath to evaporate the water, leaving solid magnesium chloride.

b **State one observation the student would see in this reaction.** (1 mark)

....

c **How would the student know that he had added excess magnesium carbonate?** (1 mark)

....

H d How many moles of HCl are there in $20\,cm^3$ of 2 mol/dm³ hydrochloric acid? (2 marks)

.... moles

H e Use the equation and your answer to (d) to calculate the volume of carbon dioxide, CO_2, produced in this reaction. If you could not answer part (d), use 0.1 moles as the amount of hydrochloric acid used. This is **not** the answer to part (d). Give your answer in dm³. (2 marks)

.... dm³

....

3.3 This experiment produced 1.18 g of magnesium chloride.

The theoretical yield of magnesium chloride in this reaction is 1.90 g.

a Calculate the percentage yield. Quote your answer to 1 decimal place. (3 marks)

....

....

b State **one** reason why the percentage yield is less than 100%. (1 mark)

....

Magnesium chloride is also formed when hydrochloric acid reacts with solid magnesium oxide.

c Write a balanced symbol equation for this reaction. Include state symbols. (3 marks)

....

3.4 Titrations can be carried out to find out the unknown concentration of solutions.

A student carried out a titration to find out the concentration of a solution of potassium hydroxide.

She placed $25\,cm^3$ of the potassium hydroxide to a conical flask and added a few drops of phenolphthalein indicator.

She then added a standard solution $0.15\,mol/dm^3$ nitric acid to the conical flask until the solution went from pink to colourless.

The equation for the reaction is as follows:

$$KOH(aq) + HNO_3(aq) \rightarrow KNO_3(aq) + H_2O(l)$$

The table below shows her results.

	Rough	2	3	4
Volume of 0.15 mol/dm³ nitric acid added/cm³	20.10	19.70	23.20	19.80

a **How many times should a titration be carried out?** (1 mark)

....

b **Calculate the mean volume of nitric acid used in the titration.** (2 marks)

....

....

c **Calculate the concentration of the potassium hydroxide, in mol/dm³.** (3 marks)

....

....

d **Calculate the concentration of the potassium hydroxide, in g/dm³.** (2 marks)
$$[K = 39, O = 16, H = 1]$$

....

....

One of the products formed in this reaction is water.

e **Name the other product.** (1 marks) ....

The reaction that takes place is a neutralisation reaction.

f **Write the ionic equation for this reaction, including state symbols.** (2 marks)

....

4.1 **Electrolysis can be used to break down ionic compounds into their elements, and is often used to extract metals from their ores.**

a **Potassium cannot be extracted from its ore using carbon. Explain why.** (1 mark)

....

....

Molten potassium chloride, KCl, consists of potassium ions and chloride ions. It undergoes electrolysis to form potassium and chlorine.

b **What is the name of the electrolyte?** (1 mark) ....

c **State the formula of the potassium ion.** (1 mark) ....

The chloride ions are attracted to the positive electrode.

H d **Complete and balance the half equation for the reaction that takes place at the positive electrode.** (1 mark)

............Cl^- → ....Cl_2^+............

e **What type of reaction is this?** (1 mark) ....

4.2 A student carried out the electrolysis of **aqueous** solutions of potassium chloride.

She was surprised to find that during the electrolysis of aqueous potassium chloride that bubbles of gas were produced at each electrode.

a Name the gas produced at the negative electrode and explain why this is formed rather than potassium. (2 marks)

....

....

H b Write a half equation for this reaction. (2 marks)

....

c What is the name of the remaining solution? (1 mark)

....

5.1 A student investigated the reactivity of four different metals by measuring the temperature change when they were reacted with hydrochloric acid. The equipment they used is shown below.

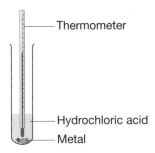

Thermometer

Hydrochloric acid
Metal

The student used the same amount of metal in each experiment.

a State **two** further variables that would need to be controlled. (2 marks)

....

b What is the **independent** variable in this reaction? (1 mark)

....

The table below shows the results of the experiment. The student concluded that the higher the temperature rise, the more reactive the metal.

Metal	Temperature change/°C
Zinc	5.5
Iron	0.5
Calcium	15.0
Magnesium	12.0

c **Place the metals in order of reactivity, from most reactive to least reactive.** (2 marks)

Most reactive	
Least reactive	

All of these reactions are **exothermic.**

d **Complete the word equation for the reaction between calcium and hydrochloric acid.**
(2 marks)

Calcium + hydrochloric acid → .... **+** ....

e **Draw a reaction profile diagram for this reaction on a separate piece of paper.** (3 marks)

H 5.2 Ethanol is a very useful fuel as it can be produced from renewable sources. It has the formula C_2H_5OH.

The equation below shows the complete combustion of ethanol.

The table below shows the bond energies of some common bonds.

Bond	Bond energy (kJ per mol)
C-C	350
C-H	415
O=O	500
C=O	800
O-H	465
C-O	360

a **Use this information to work out the energy change in this reaction.** (3 marks)

....

....

....

b **State, with a reason, if this reaction is exothermic or endothermic.** (2 marks)

....

....

For an additional Practice Paper, visit: www.scholastic.co.uk/gcse

Answers

For answers to the Practice Papers, visit:
www.scholastic.co.uk/gcse

Atomic structure and the periodic table

Atoms, elements and compounds

1 a Atom – The smallest part of an element that can exist; Element – A substance made of only one type of atom; Compound – A substance that contains two or more elements chemically combined; Mixture – A substance that contains two or more elements not chemically combined.

 b Br_2; Ar c B d 9 e 3

2 a Any two from fluorine, chlorine, bromine, iodine or astatine (must be the name, not the symbol).

 b Any two from Li, Na, K, Rb, Cs or Fr (not H as not in group 1 of the periodic table).

Mixtures and compounds

1 Element: hydrogen, oxygen; Compound: sodium hydroxide, water; Mixture: air, salty water.

2 Heat the solution; Allow water to evaporate/leave to form crystals.

3 a Condenser

 b Water boils and turns into a gas/vapour; The vapour is then cooled in the condenser and turns back into water; The salt remains in the flask as it has a higher melting/boiling point than water.

4 Any four from: Crush rock salt; Add rock salt to water; Heat/stir until NaCl dissolves; Filter to remove sand; Heat remaining solution; Leave to crystallise/allow water to evaporate.

Scientific models of the atom

1 Before the discovery of the electron, atoms were thought to be tiny spheres that could not be divided.

2 Ball/sphere of positive charge; electrons embedded in the sphere.

3 a Positive

 b Most of the atom is empty space.

 c Only part of the atom has a positive charge.

 d Mass of the atom is concentrated in the middle/nucleus; this positive charge is found in the middle of the atom/nucleus.

 e Neutrons

Atomic structure, isotopes and relative atomic mass

1

Sub-atomic particle	Relative charge	Relative mass
Proton	+1	1
Electron	−1	Very small
Neutron	0	1

2 There are equal numbers of protons and electrons/6 protons and electrons; The positive and negative charges cancel each other out.

3 a 74 protons and 74 electrons; 110 neutrons.

 b Gold (not Au)

4 atomic; mass; protons; neutrons; 6; 6; 7

5 Both isotopes have 35 protons; and 35 electrons; Br-79 has 44 neutrons and Br-81 has 46 neutrons or Br-81 has 2 more neutrons than Br-79.

6 The other isotope makes up 25%;

 $(35 \times 75) + (Cl \times 25)/100 = 35.5$;

 Cl = 37. (Final answer of 37 gains all 3 marks)

The development of the periodic table and the noble gases

1 a 4 b 4

 c Same number of electrons/5 electrons in outer shell.

 d Same number of electron shells.

2 a Periods

 b For missing/undiscovered elements.

 c By increasing atomic/proton number.

 d Because they are unreactive.

3 a Increase down the group.

 b Any number between −185 and −109.

Electronic structure

1 a Nucleus

 b Protons; and neutrons (1 mark each).

 c Aluminium or Al. d 14

2 a C b A c B, E

 d B, F e D f A

Metals and non-metals

1 Malleable – Can be hammered into shape; Ductile – Can be drawn into wires; Sonorous – Makes a ringing sound when hit.

2 a Na d Ar g Ca

 b Au e B h N

 c Si f Br

3 a Non-metal b 2

 c Good electrical conductor; shiny.

Group 1 – the alkali metals

1 They all have 1 electron in their outer shell.

2 Potassium

3 Francium

4 Na

5 Any three from: Fizzing/bubbling/effervescence, not gas given off; Lithium floats; Lithium moves on the surface; Lithium dissolves/gets smaller/disappears.

6 Any two from: Potassium melts/forms a ball; Potassium catches fire; Lilac/purple; Reaction is faster/more vigorous.

Group 7 – the halogens

1 F 2 Fluorine

3 Br_2 4 Chlorine

5 a Lithium and chlorine, as chlorine is more reactive.

 b Lithium + chlorine → lithium chloride

 c $2Li + I_2 → 2LiI$ (correct; balanced)

6 a

	Chlorine	Bromine	Iodine
Potassium chloride	x	No reaction	No reaction
Potassium bromide	Orange solution formed	x	No reaction
Potassium iodide	Brown solution formed	Brown solution formed	x

 b Chlorine + potassium bromide → bromine + potassium chloride

 c Add iodine to potassium astatide (or any astatide salt); Brown colour of iodine disappears/solution turns darker.

 $I_2 + 2At^- → 2I- + At_2$

The transition metals

1 Silver; mercury; tungsten.

2 a Any from: shiny; unreactive; hard; strong.

 b Any three from: High melting points; High density; Unreactive [if not given in (a)]; Hard [if not given in (a)]; Strong [if not given in (a)].

3 a Sodium chloride b White

 c $2Na + Cl_2 → 2NaCl$ (correct; balanced)

4 Less, as iron is less reactive.

Bonding, structure and the properties of matter

Bonding and structure

1

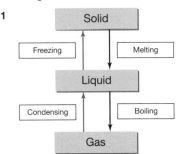

2 a 0°C **b** 100°C

3 a Gas **b** Solid

   c Liquid

4 a Oxygen **b** Nitrogen

   c Oxygen **d** Oxygen

Ions and ionic bonding

1 Magnesium is a metal which is found in group **2** of the periodic table. This means it has **2** electrons in its outer shell. When it reacts, it loses **2** oloctrons and forms an ion with a **2$^+$** charge. Fluorine is a non-metal which is found in group **7** of the periodic table. When it reacts, it **gains** 1 electron to form an ion with a **1$^-$** charge. When magnesium reacts with fluorine, it forms magnesium fluoride which has the formula **MgF$_2$**.

2 Potassium chloride, KCl; Magnesium oxide, MgO$_2$; Magnesium chloride, MgCl$_2$; Aluminium fluoride, AlF$_3$.

3 a Formula = LiCl

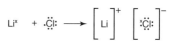

   (correct ion; correct formula)

   b Formula = BaBr$_2$

$$Ba_x^x + 2\cdot\ddot{Br}\!:\,_2 \longrightarrow \left[Ba\right]^{2+} \left[\ddot{Br}\!:\right]^-$$

   (correct ion; correct formula)

The structure and properties of ionic compounds

1 High melting points; Conduct electricity when molten or in solution; Made of ions.

2 a B **b** A **c** C

3 Ionic bonds are formed when **metals** react with **non-metals**. Atoms either lose or gain **electrons** to become positive or negative particles called ions. The ions are held together in a giant ionic **lattice** by strong **electrostatic** forces of attraction acting in all **directions**.

4 Level 1 (marks 1–2)

KI is ionic/made of ions/consists of a giant ionic lattice.

KI will have a high melting point *or* will conduct electricity when molten or in solution.

Level 2 (marks 3–4)

KI will have a high melting point because the ions are strongly attracted together/lots of energy is needed to break the strong ionic bonds *or*

KI will conduct electricity when molten or in solution/dissolved because the ions are free to move.

Level 3 (marks 5–6)

KI will have a high melting point because the ions are strongly attracted together/lots of energy is needed to break the strong ionic bonds *and*

KI will conduct electricity when molten or in solution/dissolved because the ions are free to move *and*

KI will not conduct electricity when solid as the ions do not move/are in fixed positions.

Covalent bonds and simple molecules

1 NH$_3$; Water.

2 a and **b**

Hydrogen

Formula: H$_2$

Methane

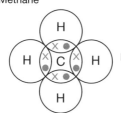

Formula: CH$_4$

3 a

   b Covalent bond – triple bond

4 a

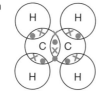

   (each single bond; correct double bond)

   b Covalent bonds – 4 × single and 1 × double

Diamond, graphite and graphene

1 a A **b** C

2 a Strong covalent bonds; large amounts of energy needed to overcome/break covalent bonds.

   b Each carbon is bonded to 4 other carbon atoms; covalent bonds are very strong.

   c Both have delocalised electrons; both conduct electricity.

3 a Does not have delocalised electrons. (do not allow free/mobile ions).

   b High melting/boiling points hard. (due to no delocalised electrons).

Fullerenes and polymers

1 a D **b** C

   c A **d** B

2 a Hollow/spherical

   b Large surface area

3 a Covalent

   b • Polyethene is a bigger molecule so has larger intermolecular forces;

     • More energy needed to overcome these intermolecular forces;

     • Increases the melting point;

     • Allow reverse argument.

Giant metallic structures and alloys

1 Metals are **giant** structures. The atoms are arranged in **layers**.

The outer shell electrons become detached from the rest of the atom and are said to be **delocalised**. This means they are free to move throughout the whole metal.

Metallic bonding is strong because of the **electrostatic** attraction between the positive metal ions and the electrons.

2 free electrons from outer shells of metal atoms

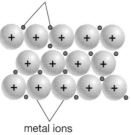

metal ions

Giant structure; Positive metal ions drawn and labelled; Delocalised electrons drawn and labelled; Electrons can carry charge throughout the metal.

3 a Strong electrostatic attraction between positive metal ions and delocalised electrons; Lots of energy needed to overcome the strong attraction.

   b Carbon/different sized atoms distort the regular lattice; Layers cannot slide over each other.

Nanoparticles

1 1–100 nm

2 a 8.6×10^{-8} m

   b 1.46×10^{-8} m

   c 1.58×10^{-7} m

   d 8.2×10^{-9} m

   e c– because the value is > 100 nm (both points needed)

3 a • Surface area = $5^2 \times 6$ = 150 nm^2; [units not needed]

     • Volume = 5^3 = 125 nm^3;

     • SA:volume ratio = 150/125 = 1.2.

   b As length of the side increases, ratio increases; by a factor of 10.

Quantitative chemistry

Conservation of mass and balancing equations

1 a Magnesium + oxygen → magnesium oxide

b Reactants: Magnesium, oxygen; Products: Magnesium oxide.

c 20 g

2 a Nitrogen + hydrogen → ammonia

b

	Reactants	Products
N	2	1
H	2	3

c $N_2(g) + 3H_2(g) → 2NH_3(g)$

3 $Fe_2O_3 + 2CO → 2Fe + 2CO_2$

Relative formula masses

1 The relative atomic mass (symbol = A_r) of an element is the weighted average mass of its naturally occurring isotopes;

You calculate the relative formula mass (symbol = M_r) of a compound by adding up all the relative atomic masses of all the atoms present in the formula of the compound;

The elements hydrogen, oxygen, nitrogen, chlorine, bromine, iodine and fluorine exist as diatomic molecules- in equations their relative formula masses are twice their relative atomic masses;

The law of mass conservation means that in a chemical reaction the sum of the relative formula masses of the reactants is equal to the sum of the relative formula mass of the products.

2 Carbon − 12; Oxygen − 16; Chlorine 35.5; Iron − 55.8

3 a NaOH − 40; H_2SO_4 − 98; Na_2SO_4 − 142; H_2O − 18

b 10 g/98 = 0.010 → 0.010 × 18 = 1.84 g

c 5 g/142 = 0.35 → 0.035 × 40 × 2 = 2.82 g

d So they know how much product will be made OR to avoid waste.

The mole and reactive masses

H 1 a 0.1 moles   b 0.1 moles

c 0.003 (or $3.125 × 10^{-3}$) moles

d 0.5 moles

H 2 a 36.5 g   b 60 g

c 31.8 g   d 171 g

H 3 a

Substance	A_r or M_r	Mass/g	Moles
sodium	23.0	2.30	0.1
sulfur	32	0.32	0.01
CH_4	16	1.60	0.1

b 1.37 moles

H 4 a 152   b 38 g

c 19 g   d $7.5 × 10^{22}$

H 5 a 14 g

b 1 136 364 (or $1.13664 × 10^6$) g

H 6 a 0.003 moles   b 0.02 moles

c $2.29 × 10^{23}$

Limiting reactants

H 1 a Hydrochloric acid

b Magnesium

H 2 How many moles of water can be produced by 1 mole of H_2? 1

How many moles of water can be produced by 1 mole of O_2? 2

Which is the limiting reactant? H_2

How much H_2O is produced in the reaction? 1

Which reactant is in excess? O_2

How many moles of O_2 is used in the reaction? 1

H 3 a $4Cu + O_2 → 2Cu_2O$

b Cu → 1.26 moles; O_2 → 1.56 moles

c Copper; because in the equation, the ratio of moles is Cu:O_2 4:1, however in the experiment there was only 1.26:1.56 moles.

H 4 a $C_3H_8 + 5O_2 → 3CO_2 + 4H_2O$

b 5.68 g

c The limiting reactant is oxygen; because in the balanced equation the ratio is 1:5 (0.3:1.5), but the engine only has 0.3:0.1; they could make the engine more efficient by increasing the amount of oxygen.

Concentrations in solutions

H 1 a 1   b 2

H 2 a Test 1 − 250 g/dm³

Test 2 − 400 g/dm³

Test 3 − 571 g/dm³

b Test 1 − 0.09 moles

Test 2 − 0.17 moles

Test 3 − 0.34 moles

H 3 a 143

b 0.01 moles/143 g/mol = 1.43 g = 1.43 g/dm³

c 3 575 000 g; $3.575 × 10^6$ g

Moles in solution

H 1 a 0.25 moles   b 10 mol/dm⁻³

H 2 0.05 mol/dm⁻³

H 3 1 260 mol/dm⁻³

Moles and gas volumes

H 1 At the same temperature and pressure equal **volumes** of different gases contain the same number of molecules.

This means that under the same conditions, equal volumes of gases have the same number of **moles** present.

At room temperature (20°C) and atmospheric pressure, together known as **room temperature and pressure (RTP)**, 1 mole of any gas occupies a volume of 24 dm³.

H 2 144 dm³

H 3 a 83.3 moles   b 0.083 moles

c 3.66 g

Percentage yield and atom economy

1 a

$$\frac{\text{Relative formula mass of desired product}}{\text{Sum of relative formula masses of reactants}} × 100$$

b They would understand how much of the desired product is made from the reactants and how much is wasted; it can inform decisions about the sustainability of different methods/percentage yield gives no information about the quantity of wasted atoms.

c 1 $\frac{48}{128} × 100 = 38\%$

2 $\frac{48}{80} × 100 = 60\%$

d It would increase the atom economy of method (2) to 100%; making method (2) even more favourable.

2 a $CaCO_3 = 100$; CaO = 56

b 56%

c 7 g

d $\frac{6.5}{7} × 100 = 92.9\%$

Chemical changes

Metal oxides and the reactivity series

1 a Magnesium + oxygen → magnesium oxide

b $2Mg(s) + O_2(g) → 2MgO(s)$ (correct; balanced)

c Oxygen is gained/electrons are lost.

2 a Aluminium + lead chloride → aluminium chloride + lead

b Silver + copper oxide → no reaction

c Calcium + zinc nitrate → calcium nitrate + zinc

d Iron chloride + copper → no reaction

3 a 1-Sodium, 2-X, 3-Magnesium, 4-Copper.

b Copper

Extraction of metals and reduction

1 Carbon is less reactive than magnesium.

2 It's unreactive/doesn't easily form compounds.

3 a Copper oxide + carbon → carbon oxide/dioxide + copper (reactants; products)

b Carbon

4 a Reduction/redox

b $2Fe_2O_3(s) + 3C(s) \rightarrow 4Fe(l) + 3CO_2(g)$ (reactants; products)

c Iron is a liquid.

d Carbon is more reactive than iron.

e Any metal above iron in the reactivity series; Too expensive/metals above carbon extracted by electrolysis so require more energy.

The reactions of acids

1 Both neutralise acid; Bases are insoluble/alkalis are soluble bases/alkalis form hydroxide/OH⁻ ions ins solution.

2 **a** Sodium chloride – sodium hydroxide and hydrochloric acid.

b Potassium nitrate – potassium carbonate and nitric acid.

c Copper sulfate – copper oxide and sulfuric acid.

3 **a** Solid dissolves/colourless solution forms.

b Fizzing occurs with magnesium carbonate.

c Magnesium oxide + hydrochloric acid → magnesium chloride + water

d $MgCO_3$

4 **a** $Mg(s) + 2HCl(aq) \rightarrow MgCl_2(aq) + H_2(g)$

b $Li_2O(s) + H_2SO_4(aq) \rightarrow Li_2SO_4(aq) + H_2O(l)$

c $CuO(s) + 2HCl(aq) \rightarrow CuCl_2(aq) + H_2O(l)$

5 **a** $Ca(s) + 2H^+(aq) \rightarrow Ca^{2+}(aq) + H_2(g)$ (reactants; products; state symbols)

b Ca oxidised; H^+/hydrogen reduced.

The preparation of soluble salts

1 **a** Copper carbonate + sulfuric acid → copper sulfate + water + carbon dioxide

b Any two from: Copper carbonate dissolves; Fizzing/bubbles/effervescence; Blue/green solution forms.

c To ensure all the acid reacts.

d Filtration

e Copper oxide/copper hydroxide.

f Any one from: Salt lost from spitting during evaporation; Solution left in container; Not all the solution crystallises.

2 **a** $Ca(s) + 2HNO_3(aq) \rightarrow Ca(NO_3)_2(aq) + H_2(g)$ (reactants; products; state symbols)

b % yield = 2.6/3.0 x 100; 87.7%

3 **Possible steps to include:**
Reactants (zinc/zinc hydroxide/zinc oxide/zinc carbonate) and hydrochloric acid; Correct equation for chosen reactants; Heat acid; Add base until no more reacts/dissolves so the base is in <u>excess</u>; Filter unreacted base; Heat solution on a steam bath until half the water has evaporated; Leave remaining solution to cool so crystals form.

Equipment list: Bunsen burner; Heatproof mat; Tripod; Gauze; Beaker; Evaporating dish; Funnel; Filter paper; Conical flask; Spatula; Measuring cylinder; Safety glasses.

Oxidation and reduction in terms of electrons

1 **a** $Mg(s) + Cu^{2+}(aq) \rightarrow Mg^{2+}(aq) + Cu(s)$

b Mg is oxidised and Cu is reduced.

2 **a** $Mg(s) + Zn^{2+}(aq) \rightarrow Mg^{2+}(aq) + Zn(s)$; Mg oxidised, Zn reduced.

b $2Na(s) + Zn^{2+}(aq) \rightarrow 2Na^+(aq) + Zn(s)$; Na oxidised, Zn reduced.

c $Cu(s) + 2Ag^+(aq) \rightarrow Cu^{2+}(aq) + 2Ag(s)$; Cu oxidised, Zn reduced.

d $3Ca(s) + 2Fe^{3+}(aq) \rightarrow 3Ca^{2+}(aq) + 2Fe(s)$; Ca oxidised, Fe reduced.

pH scale and neutralisation

1 Strong acid – pH 2 – Red, Weak acid – pH 5 – Yellow, Strong alkali – pH 13 – Purple, Weak alkali - pH 9 – Blue, Neutral – pH 7 – Green.

2 Hydroxide ion

3 H^+

4 pH 1

5 pH 12

6 **a** Potassium hydroxide.

b $2KOH + H_2SO_4 \rightarrow K_2SO_4 + 2H_2O$

c $H^+ + OH^- \rightarrow H_2O$ **or** $2H^+ + 2OH^- \rightarrow 2H_2O$

7 OH^- and NH_4^+

Strong and weak acids

1 **a** $HNO_3(aq) \rightarrow H^+(aq) + NO_3^-(aq)$

b $HCOOH(aq) \rightarrow H^+(aq) + COO^-(aq)$

c $H_2SO_4(aq) \rightarrow 2H^+(aq) + SO_4^{2-}(aq)$ **or** $H_2SO_4(aq) \rightarrow H^+(aq) + HSO_4^-(aq)$

2 Weak acid only partially ionises in solution; Dilute acid has fewer moles of solute dissolved.

3 **a** 1×10^{-3}

b Answer is 100 times greater as if pH decreases by 1, H^+ concentration increases by 10; 0.1 (overrides previous mark); 1×10^{-1}

Electrolysis

1

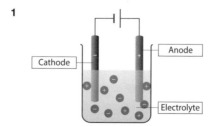

2 Ions are free to move when molten/aqueous; Ions in fixed positions/ions can't move in solid lattice.

3 **a** Zinc and chlorine.

b Silver and iodine.

c Copper and oxygen.

4 **a** $Pb^{2+} + 2e^- \rightarrow Pb$; $2Br^- \rightarrow Br_2 + 2e^-$

b Lead/lead ions reduced and bromine/bromide ions oxidised.

The electrolysis of aqueous solutions

1 **a** Copper chloride – copper and chlorine.

b Potassium bromide – hydrogen and bromine.

c Zinc sulfate – zinc and oxygen.

d Sodium carbonate – hydrogen and oxygen.

2 **a** $2H^+ + 2e^- \rightarrow H_2$

b Chlorine; $2Cl^- \rightarrow Cl_2 + 2e^-$ (correct; balanced)

3 **a** H^+/hydrogen; Li^+/lithium; OH^-/hydroxide.

b I^-/iodide ions attracted to anode/positive electrode; Lose electron/an electron; Form iodine; $2I^- \rightarrow I_2 + 2e^-$.

c Lithium hydroxide/LiOH.

4 **a** Anode

b $4OH^- \rightarrow O_2 + 2H_2O + 4e^-$; OH^- and H_2O (correct; balanced)

The extraction of metals using electrolysis

1 **a** Strong ionic bonds/strong electrostatic attraction between oppositely charged ions; Requires lots of energy to overcome.

b So the ions are free to move.

c Reduce the operating temperature; Saves energy/reduces energy costs.

d Electrons are lost.

e $Al^{3+} + 3e^- \rightarrow Al$ (correct; balanced electrons)

f They react with the oxygen produced; Carbon + oxygen → carbon dioxide/$C + O_2 \rightarrow CO_2$

g Electricity wasn't discovered/electricity not needed to extract iron.

Practical investigation into the electrolysis of aqueous solutions

1 **a** Independent – Metal/metal ion in salt; Dependent variable – Product formed at cathode; Control variables – Volume of solution, Concentration of solution, Negative ion in salt, Voltages.

b Only 1 variable is changed.

2 Place a lighted splint into the gas; Positive test – burns with a squeaky pop.

3 **a** $CuCl_2$ – Copper; all others – Hydrogen.

b Solutions containing metals above hydrogen in the reactivity series produce hydrogen on electrolysis; Solutions containing metals below hydrogen in the reactivity series produce the metal on electrolysis.

4 Chlorine; Bleaches blue litmus paper **or** bleaches UI in solution.

Titrations

1 a Titre 1: 14.90 cm³ ; Titre 2: 15.35 cm³; Titre 3: 14.80 cm³ (3 correct 2 marks, 2 correct 1 mark. Must be to 2 decimal places.)

b 14.85 (2 marks as outlier ignored); 15.02 (1 mark if outlier included)

c Until consistent results/two titres within 0.10 cm³

2

Volume NaOH (cm³)	Concentration NaOH (mol/dm³)	Volume HCl (cm³)	Concentration HCl (mol/dm³)
25.00	0.1	25.00	0.1
25.00	0.1	50.00	**0.05**
12.50	0.2	**25.00**	0.1
20.00	0.5	10.00	**1.0**

3 **Possible steps to include:** Use of pipette to measure out alkali; Place this solution into a conical flask; Add an indicator; Place conical flask onto a white tile; Fill burette with acid; Carry out rough titration; Add acid to alkali until there is a colour change; Record readings to nearest 0.05cm³; Repeat, slowing down addition of acid when close to rough titration reading; Continue until consistent results obtained/two results within 0.10 cm³ of each other.

Equipment: Conical flask; Pipette (and filler); Burette; White tile; Indicator.

4 a Moles NaOH = conc × vol = 0.1 × 0.025 = 0.0025; moles HNO₃ = 0.0025; Conc HNO₃ = moles/vol = 0.0025/0.0216 = 0.116 mol/dm³

b Formula mass HNO₃ = 63; Conc HNO₃ = 63 x 0.116 = 7.29 g/dm³

5 a 2KOH + H₂SO₄ → K₂SO₄ + 2H₂O

b i Moles KOH = conc x vol = 0.2 x 0.025 = 0.005; moles H₂SO₄ = 0.005 x 2 = 0.0025; Conc H₂SO₄ = moles/vol = 0.0025/0.0145 = 0.172 mol/dm³

ii Formula mass H₂SO₄ = 98; Conc HNO₃ = 98 × 0.172 = s16.9 g/dm³

(Allow error carried forward from an incorrect calculation.)

Energy changes

Exothermic and endothermic reactions

1 a Endothermic – surrounding temperatures decrease as heat energy is needed by the reaction.

b Exothermic – surrounding temperatures increase as heat energy is released by the reaction.

2 a 15.4°C − 23.7°C = −8.3. The reaction is endothermic as the temperature decrease.

b i 37°C − 25°C = +12

ii Exothermic

Practical investigation into the variables that affect temperature changes in chemical reactions

1 a

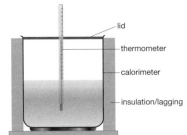

b To reduce heat loss; to give a more accurate result.

c Two from: The reaction of iron and oxygen is exothermic; The temperature increase is greatest with iron filings; Iron filings are more reactive.

d To make it a fair test; oxygen may be controlling the rate of reaction.

2 **Possible steps to include:** Use an insulated calorimeter; to reduce heat loss; use a thermometer to record temperature; use same equipment throughout; use hydrochloric acid at different concentrations; use same volume of hydrochloric acid; same volume of calcium carbonate; same particle size of calcium carbonate; to ensure a fair test; temperature increase will increase with concentration; because the rate of reaction will increase; record data on a table –

	Concentration 1	Concentration 2	Concentration 3
Initial temperature / °C			
Final temperature / °C			

Reaction profiles

1 A **reaction profile** shows how the energy changes from reactants to products

In a reaction profile for an **exothermic** reaction the products are lower in energy than the reactants because **energy** is released to the surroundings during the reaction.

In a reaction profile for an **endothermic** reaction the **products** are higher in energy than the **reactants** because energy is taken in from the **surroundings** during the reaction.

Chemical reactions occur when reacting particles collide with enough energy to react. This energy is called the **activated energy** (Ea).

2 a Products are higher in energy that reactants; the student is incorrect; the reaction is endothermic.

b i A Activation energy.

ii B Energy absorbed from surroundings.

c Catalyst reduces the activation energy:

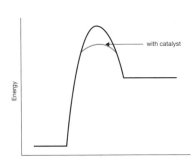

The energy changes of reactions

H 1 a H–H = 436 kJ

Cl-Cl = 243

Sum (bond breaking): 436+243 = 679 kJ

b 2 × 432 = 864 kJ

c Exothermic

d 864 − 679 = 185

H 2 a 2x (H-Br) → H-H + Br-Br

b Reactants = 366 × 2 = -732 kJ (breaking).
Products = 432 + 193 = + 625 (making).
625–732 = −107kJ = Endothermic.

Chemical cells and fuel cells

1 a Zinc

b Lemon juice/citric acid

c

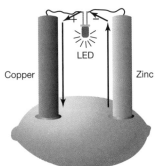

2 9/1.5 = 6 cells

3 a Electrolysis

b

Chemical cells	Fuel Cells
Can be used anywhere.	Hampered by the need for hydrogen containers.
When non-rechargeable batteries run out, they have to be thrown away and sent to recycling centre.	These will continue to work as long as the hydrogen flows.
Re-chargeable batteries can be charged again and again.	The product of the reaction is water.
Some of the metals used are toxic.	The hydrogen is flammable.

H c At the negative electrode of the fuel cell hydrogen reacts with hydroxide ions to produce water and electrons.

$2H_2(g) + 4OH^-(aq) \rightarrow 4H_2O(l) + 4e^-$

At the positive electrode oxygen gains electrons and reacts with water to produce hydroxide ions.

$O_2(g) + 2H_2O(l) + 4e^- \rightarrow 4OH^-(aq)$

Rates of reaction and equilibrium

Ways to follow a chemical reaction

1 a Size of marble chips.
  b Time
  c Volume of carbon dioxide given off (if collected); OR change in mass (if carbon dioxide allowed to escape); OR time for marble chips to disappear (if excess hydrochloric acid).
  d Two from: Mass of marble chips; volume of acid; Concentration of acid; Amount of stirring; Temperature.

2 a Production of sulfur, S, which makes the solution opaque.
  b Concentration of sodium thiosulfate.
  c Two from: Volume of sodium thiosulfate; Volume of acid; Concentration of acid; Amount of stirring; Temperature; Same person doing the timing.
  d Could use a light meter and a lamp; to reduce uncertainty about whether the x is visible or not.

3 Possible steps to include: Measure a fixed volume of (e.g. 50 cm³) of hydrochloric acid; using one of the measuring cylinders and pour it into the conical flask; Put a bung in the conical flask with a delivery tube which goes into an upturned measuring cylinder which is full of water and in a water trough; this allows me to measure the amount of hydrogen gas given off; Cut the magnesium into pieces the same size; put one piece into the conical flask; start the timer; record the amount of hydrogen gas at

regular intervals on a table; Repeat for different concentrations of hydrochloric acid.

Calculating the rate of reaction

1 Rate of reaction = Amount of product formed/Time taken

2 a The rate of reaction is constant
  b The rate of reaction is constant
  c The rate of reaction decreases with time
  d The rate of reaction increases with time

3 a $Mg + 2HCl \rightarrow MgCl_2 + H_2$
  b 99/120 = 0.825 cm³/second
  c

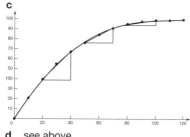

  d see above.

H e 30s = 1.8 cm³/s (Allow +/− 0.2)
  60s = 0.75 cm³/s (Allow +/− 0.2)
  90s = 0.15 cm³/s (Allow +/− 0.2)

H f 30s – from graph: 1.8 cm³/s;
  110/24 = 0.75 moles/s
  60s – from graph: 0.75 cm³/s;
  168/24 = 0.03125 moles/s

The effect of concentration and on reaction rate and the effect of pressure on the rate of gaseous reactions

1 For a reaction to happen, particles must **collide** with sufficient **energy**. The minimum amount of **energy** that particles must have for a specific reaction is known as the **activation energy**. The rate of a reaction can be increased by increasing the **energy** of collisions and increasing the **frequency** of collisions.

2 There are more particles; The frequency of successful collisions increases.

3 a C **b** A

4 a

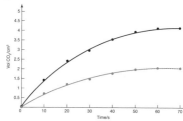

  b Rate of reaction starts off fast; slows down as the reaction progresses.
  c One (or more) of the reactants has been used up.
  d see above (light grey line)

e There are half as many hydrochloric acid particles; reducing the frequency of successful collisions; reducing the rate of reaction.

Rates of reaction – the effect of surface area

1 a B **b** B
  c More particles exposed to the other reactant; increasing the frequency of collisions.
  d Sugar is used to make marshmallows; sugar has a larger surface area; the rate of reaction with oxygen under heat would be much higher.

2 a Cut tablets; grind into powder using a pestle and mortar.
  b see graph

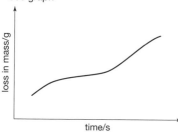

  c Collect carbon dioxide bubbles in upturned measuring cylinder; allow carbon dioxide to escape and measure mass change.

The effects of changing the temperature and adding a catalyst

1 a The particles have more energy so they collide more frequently; and with more energy
  b 10°C increase ~doubles rate. So at 30°C= 20 s. 40°C = 10 s.

2 a It is a catalyst.
  b It provides an alternative route for the reaction; reducing the activation energy.
  c

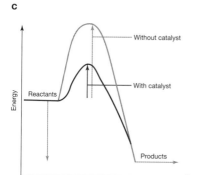

3 a Collect oxygen given off in an upturned measuring cylinder.
  b **Possible steps to include:** Put hydrogen peroxide in a test tube; Use the same volume and concentration for both tests; Put a bung at the top of the test tube with a delivery tube to an upturned measuring cylinder; Add a quantity of liver to the hydrogen peroxide; Record the volume of oxygen

Answers

produced at intervals; Repeat with the same mass of manganese oxide.

An investigation into how changing the concentration affects the rate of reaction

1   a $2HCl(aq) + Na_2S_2O_3(aq) \rightarrow 2NaCl(aq) + SO_2(g) + S(s) + H_2O(l)$

b   As the concentration increases, the rate of reaction will increase.

c   The hypothesis will be confirmed/ as the concentration increases the rate of reaction will increase; there will be more particles; more frequent collisions.

d   **Possible steps to include:**
Measure out the same volume of different concentrations of sodium thiosulfate /hydrochloric acid into conical flasks; Measure out a volume of hydrochloric acid/sodium thiosulfate; Using the same volume and concentration throughout; To ensure a fair test; Mark a cross on a sheet of white paper; Put conical flask on cross; Mix reactants; Record the time it takes for the cross to disappear; Repeat for other concentrations.

e   Temperature would increase the frequency and energy of collisions; increasing the rate of reaction.

f   Cross to disappear – easy and convenient/requires no special equipment; but can be subjective (it is down to an individual's opinion).

Lamp and light sensor – more accurate; because it is not dependent on an individual's opinion; requires additional equipment.

2   a
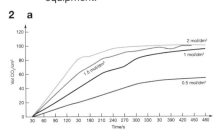

b $0.5mol/dm^3 = 0.113 \; cm^3/s$
$1mol/dm^3 = 0.198 \; cm^3/s$
$1.5mol/dm^3 = 0.222 \; cm^3/s$
$2mol/dm^3 = 0.256 \; cm^3/s$

Reversible reactions

1   a $\rightleftharpoons$

b   Reversible reactions can go both forwards and backwards in certain conditions.

c   A dynamic equilibrium is when the rate of the forward reaction is equal to the rate of the backward reaction; the concentration of the reactants and products remains constant.

2   a   A reversible reaction is one which can go both ways. This means that as well as reactants forming products, the products can also react to give the reactants.

b   Exothermic; the forward reaction requires heat so is endothermic; the backwards reaction is always the opposite of the forwards reaction.

c   The reversible reaction has reached dynamic equilibrium; both reactions are occurring at the same rate; there is no net change in the volume of carbon dioxide.

The effect of changing conditions on equilibrium

H 1   At dynamic equilibrium, the rate of the forward reaction is the same as the backward reaction.

H 2   Temperature; pressure; concentration.

H 3   If a chemical system is at equilibrium and one or more of the three conditions is changed; then the position of equilibrium will shift so as to cancel out the change; and we get either more reactants or more products.

H 4   a   The reaction would shift to the left; because the forward reaction is exothermic as it gives out heat; producing more nitrogen and hydrogen gas.

b   The forward reaction needs enough energy to overcome the activation energy or the rate of reaction will be too slow.

c   It provides an alternative route for the reaction – reducing the activation energy; and increasing the rate of reaction; meaning the reaction can be run at the lowest possible temperature which reduces the backward reaction (a compromise temperature).

d   There are fewer moles of gas in the products; increasing pressure therefore increases the forwards reaction.

Organic chemistry

Alkanes

1   a   They are molecules that contain *only* hydrogen and carbon.

b   They only contain C-C single bonds.

c   Any two from: They have similar chemical properties; They have the same general formula; Each member differs by CH_2; Same trend in physical properties.

2   a $C_{20}H_{42}$

b C_8H_{18}

3

(Correct C-H bonds; Correct C-C bond)

4   a
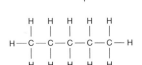

b C_7H_{16}

5   CH_4

6   Pentane

7   C_4H_{10}

Fractional distillation

1   Any 4 from: Crude oil heated; Crude oil evaporates; Vapour rises up fractionating column; Fractions with lower boiling points rise further up column/Temperature gradient in column (hotter at the bottom, cooler at the top); When vapour cools to boiling point of fractions molecules condense into a liquid; Statement relating to bigger molecules having higher boiling points.

2   a   Fuel for aeroplanes

b $C_{12}H_{26}$

c   Bigger molecules so greater intermolecular forces; More energy is needed to overcome these forces.

3   a $C_2H_6 + 3\frac{1}{2} O_2 \rightarrow 2CO_2 + 3H_2O$

b $C_3H_8 + 5O_2 \rightarrow 3CO_2 + 4H_2O$

c $C_5H_{12} + 8O_2 \rightarrow 5CO_2 + 6H_2O$
(correct; balanced)

Cracking and alkenes

1   Contain a C=C bond; Molecules made of only carbon and hydrogen.

2   a   i
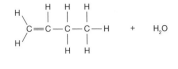

ii
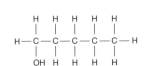

iii Propene + Chlorine

$$H_2C=CH-CH_3 + Cl_2$$

↓

$$CH_2Cl-CHCl-CH_3$$

b Only one product/no waste products.

3 a $C_8H_{18} \rightarrow C_5H_{12} + \mathbf{C_3H_6}$

b $C_{18}H_{38} \rightarrow C_3H_6 + \mathbf{C_{15}H_{32}}$

c $\mathbf{C_{13}H_{28}} \rightarrow C_4H_8 + C_9H_{20}$

d $C_{14}H_{30} \rightarrow C_4H_{10} + C_6H_{12} + \mathbf{C_4H_8}$

e $C_{14}H_{30} \rightarrow C_8H_{18} + \mathbf{2C_3H_6}$

4 a $C_{10}H_{22}$ **b** Fuel/petrol

c It's an alkene.

d Polymers

e $C_{10}H_{22} \rightarrow C_6H_{14} + C_4H_8$

Alcohols

1 a B **b** D **c** A **d** C **e** B

2 a Methanol + oxygen → carbon dioxide + water; $CH_3OH + 3/2O_2 \rightarrow CO_2 + 2H_2O$

b Propanol + oxygen → carbon dioxide + water; $CH_3CH_2CH_2OH + 9/2O_2 \rightarrow 3CO_2 + 4H_2O$
(multiples allowed)

3 a Fizzing; sodium dissolves/disappears.

b Dissolves/forms a colourless solution/miscible.

c Acidified potassium dichromate turns green.

Carboxylic acids

1 a E **b** A **c** C
d B **e** D **f** C

2 a $C_8H_{16}O_2$

b $C_3H_6O_2$; Propanoic acid.

3 HCl is a strong acid; CH_3COOH is a weak acid; HCl fully ionises; CH_3COOH only partially ionises; $HCl \rightarrow H^+ + Cl^-$ or $CH_3COOH \rightleftharpoons CH_3COO^- + H^+$

Addition polymerisation

1

Monomer	Repeating unit	Name of polymer
$H_2C=CH_2$ Ethene	$-[CH_2-CH_2]_n-$	Polyethene
$H_2C=CHCl$ Chloroethene	$-[CH_2-CHCl]_n-$	Polychloroethene

Monomer	Repeating unit	Name of polymer
$H_2C=CHOH$ Ethenol	$-[CH_2-CHOH]_n-$	Polyethenol
$H_2C=CH-C_2H_5$ Butene	$-[CH_2-CH(C_2H_5)]_n-$	Polybutene

2

Repeating unit	Monomer
$-[CH_2-CHF]_n-$	$H_2C=CHF$
$-[CHCl-CHBr]_n-$	$ClHC=CHBr$

3 a

$$n\ H_2C=CH-C_3H_7 \rightarrow -[CH_2-CH(C_3H_7)]_n-$$

(Correct repeating unit; 'n' on both sides.)

b Polypentene

Condensation polymerisation

H 1 a A and D **b** C
c Alcohol **d** Carboxylic acid

H 2 a

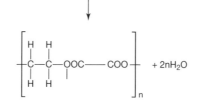

(reactants; repeating unit; all 'n' in correct places)

b Water/waste product is formed.

H 3

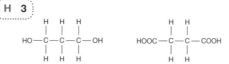

Amino acids and DNA

1 Two amino acids can join together by **condensation** polymerisation to form polypeptides and **proteins**.

Each amino acid contains two functional groups, a **carboxylic** acid group which has the formula –COOH and an amine group, which has the formula $-NH_2$. The –COOH on one amino acid reacts with the $-NH_2$ group on another amino acid forming a polymer, with the elimination of **water**.

2 a $n\ H_2NCH(CH_3)COOH \rightarrow (-HNCH(CH_3)COO-)_n + nH_2O$
(products; reactants)

b $n\ H_2NCH_2COOH + n\ H_2NCH(CH_3)COOH \rightarrow (-HNCH_2CONHCH(CH_3)COO-)n + 2nH_2O$
(reactants; 'n'; correct product with peptide link)

3 Nucleotides

4 Sugars

Chemical analysis

Pure substances and formulations

1 Pure substances are either single elements or single compounds.

2 a Although milk doesn't contain additives; it is a mixture of compounds.

b You could heat the mixture and using a thermometer; observe a range of boiling points; pure substances have a specific boiling/melting point. (No mark for 'separate the mixture'.)

3 It is not pure – it contains other elements or compounds.

4 a

Pure water vapour
Salt water
Heat
Pure water

b The salt water is heated; water boils at 100°C; the water vapour rises up the round-bottomed flask and enters a condenser where it cools and turns into a liquid; the salt is left behind as it boils at a higher temperature.

5 a A formulation is a mixture that is designed to be an improvement on the activate substance on its own – the lubricant stops the paracetamol sticking/makes it easier to swallow.

b 0.5g + 0.25g + 1.25g = 2g
0.5g/2g = 0.25 × 100 = 25%

H c i Paracetamol = 151 → 0.5/151
= 0.003 moles or 3×10^{-3} moles

ii Starch = 162 → 1.25/162
= 0.008 moles or 8×10^{-3} moles

iii Magnesium stearate = 591 → 0.25/591 = 0.0004 moles or 4×10^{-4} moles

d 0.003 + 0.008 + 0.004 = 0.0114.
0.003/0.0114 × 100 = 26.3%

Chromatography

1 Chromatography is a technique that can be used to separate mixtures into their components; Chromatography works because different compounds have different levels of attraction for the paper and the solvent.

2 a Water line is above the base line; which will cause the inks to disperse in the water rather than up the paper; The base line is drawn in ink; which may contain colours that could contaminate the chromatogram/which could interfere with the experiment.

b R_f = distance travelled/solvent front = 22/25 = 0.88. C is yellow.

Testing for gases

1 Hydrogen – a lighted splint put into a test tube of the gas – is extinguished with a 'pop';
Oxygen – a glowing splint put into a test tube of the gas – Relights;
Carbon dioxide – bubble the gas through a solution of limewater – produces solid calcium carbonate, turning the limewater cloudy.

2 a The gas turns limewater turns cloudy **Carbon dioxide**

b The gas bleaches litmus paper **Chlorine**

c The gas extinguishes a lighted splint with a pop **Hydrogen**

d The gas relights a glowing splint **Oxygen**

3 a $CH_4 + 2O_2 \rightarrow CO_2 + 2H_2O$ Bubble through limewater – would turn cloudy.

b $Mg + H_2SO_4 \rightarrow MgSO_4 + H_2A$ lighted splint put into the gas – extinguishes with a pop.

c $CO_2 + H_2O \rightarrow C_6H_{12}O_6 + O_2$ A glowing splint put into the gas – will reignite.

d $HCl + MnO_2 \rightarrow MnCl_2 + 2H_2O + Cl_2$ Litmus paper when exposed to the gas – will bleach.

4 Carbon dioxide gas produced so the limewater will turn cloudy; because it is a combustion reaction involving a fuel and oxygen.
Description of different tests for each gas: hydrogen – lit splint in flame/ oxygen – glowing splint will reignite/ chlorine – bleaches litmus paper; these tests will be negative.

Identifying metal ions using flame tests, flame emission spectroscopy and sodium hydroxide

1 Lithium carbonate – Crimson; Sodium chloride – Yellow; Potassium sulfate – Lilac; Calcium nitrate – Orange-red; Copper phosphate – Green.

2 a Lithium; Sodium.

b i

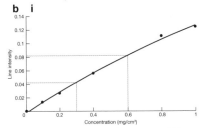

ii 0.3 moles/cm³ (accept within 2 d.p.)

iii Line intensity 0.0.82 (accept within 2 d.p.)

Testing for negative ions (anions) in salts

1
Chloride (Cl⁻)
Nitric acid followed by silver nitrate solution
White precipitate (of silver chloride);

Bromide (Br⁻)
Nitric acid followed by silver nitrate solution
Cream precipitate (of silver bromide);

Iodide (I⁻)
Nitric acid followed by silver nitrate solution
Yellow precipitate (of silver iodide);

Sulfate (SO_4^{2-})
Hydrochloric acid followed by barium chloride solution
White precipitate (of barium sulfate);

Carbonate (CO_3^{2-})
Hydrochloric acid then pass gas formed through limewater
Effervescence and gas turns limewater cloudy/milky.

2 a Carbonate was present; chloride was present from the sodium chloride.

b Hydrochloric acid contains chloride ions; this would give a positive reading to test; regardless of the contents of the salt.

c Silver chloride.

H d $2H^+(aq) + CO_3^{2-}(s) \rightarrow CO_2(g) + H_2O(l)$

Identifying ions in an ionic compound

1 a Flame test – calcium gives red flame, lithium gives crimson; OR add sodium hydroxide, if white precipitate forms it is calcium.

b Nitric acid followed by silver nitrate solution; chloride gives white precipitate, bromide gives cream.

2 Positive ion: Flame test – yellow flame if sodium present; Negative ion: Hydrochloric acid followed by barium chloride solution; White precipitate if sulfate present.

3 A – Potassium carbonate; B – Lithium sulfate; C – Aluminium bromide; D – Iron(III) iodide.

4 Hydrochloric acid + calcium carbonate → calcium chloride + carbon dioxide + water; Flame test – brick red; Nitric acid followed by silver nitrate solution; gives white precipitate.

Chemistry of the atmosphere

The composition and evolution of the Earth's atmosphere

1 a Carbonate rock formation; Fossil fuel formation.

b Condensation/formation of oceans OR used in photosynthesis by plants.

c It reduced; carbon dioxide dissolved in the oceans.

d $6CO_2 + 6H_2O \rightarrow C_6H_{12}O_6 + 6O_2$ (correct; balanced)

2 a $2Cu + O_2 \rightarrow 2CuO$

b 21.5%

c To make sure no other variables were affecting the results; to reduce error.

Global warming

1 a Climate is complex **or** models are simplifications.

b Results of experiments are checked by other scientists.

c Carbon dioxide; methane; water vapour.

d Any four from: Carbon dioxide – burning fossil fuels in our homes/ industry/cars; deforestation;
Methane – cattle farming; rice crops; landfill;
Water – small increases from farming and burning fossil fuels, most is due to natural evaporation; higher global temperatures increases the rate of evaporation.

2 a Temperature increases at the same time as CO_2 increases; There is a big increase in temperatures more recently.

b The graph shows a correlation between CO_2 and temperature; it is known that human activity has increase atmospheric CO_2; it is known that CO_2 is a greenhouse gas; recent temperatures are much higher than in the past.

The carbon footprint and its reduction

1   Alternative energy – Renewable energy sources such as solar cells, wind power and wave power do not rely on the burning of fossil fuels;

Energy conservation – Reducing the amount of energy used by using energy-saving measures such as house insulation, using devices that use less energy, reduces the demand for energy;

Carbon Capture and Storage (CCS) – Removing the carbon dioxide given out by power stations by reacting it with other chemicals. The product of this reaction can then be stored deep under the sea in porous sedimentary rocks;

Carbon taxes – Penalising companies and individuals who use too much energy by increasing their taxes reduces the demand for energy;

Carbon offsetting – Removing carbon dioxide from the air using natural biological processes such as photosynthesis. This is achieved by planting trees and increasing marine algae by adding chemicals to the oceans.;

Using plants as biofuels – Plants take in carbon dioxide as they grow, when they are burned they only release the same amount of carbon dioxide. This makes them carbon neutral.

2   a   Any two from: High use of cars/preference for large cars; developed countries use more energy; high level of industrialisation in USA and Qatar; China and India and developing countries.

b   It has **reduced** from 10 tonnes per person to 7.1 tonnes per person.

c   Increase in population; increase in industry; increased development has resulted in greater energy use.

Atmospheric pollutants

1

Soot	Global dimming and lung damage	Ensure complete combustion of fossil fuels
Carbon monoxide	A toxic gas which binds to haemoglobin in the blood, preventing the transport of oxygen around the body	Ensure complete combustion of fossil fuels
Sulfur dioxide	Dissolves in clouds to cause acid rain and causes respiratory problems	Desulfurisation of petrochemicals before combustion
Oxides of nitrogen	Dissolves in clouds to cause acid rain and causes respiratory problems	Catalytic converters used after combustion

2   a   Petrol emits more carbon dioxide/ diesel emits less carbon dioxide; diesel emits four times more sulfur dioxide; diesel emits particulate matter, petrol does not; diesel emits slightly more oxides of nitrogen.

b   Any two from: Energy and materials are used in construction and transport of vehicles; energy is required to power the vehicles; this energy comes from electricity; which may be produced by burning fossil fuels.

H 3 a   Complete combustion = CH4 + 2O2 → CO2 + 2H2O, therefore:

i $CH_4 + 1\frac{1}{2} O_2 \rightarrow CO + 2H_2O$

ii $CH_4 + O_2 \rightarrow C + 2H_2O$

b   When 4 moles of coal are burned, 960 moles of carbon dioxide are produced; therefore, 960/4 = 240 moles of carbon dioxide per mole of coal. 240 × 8 = 1920 moles of carbon dioxide.

c   Burning coal produces nitric acid (HNO_3) and sulfuric acid (H_2SO_4); causing acid rain which is corrosive/reacts with limestone.

Using resources

Finite and renewable resources, sustainable development

1   The **natural resources** used by chemists to make new materials can be divided into two categories – **finite** and **renewable**. **Finite** resources will run out. Examples are fossil fuels and various metals. **Renewable** resources are ones that can be replaced at the same rate as they are used up. They are derived from plant materials.

Sustainable development meets the needs of present development without depleting natural resources for future generations.

2   Have reactions with high atom economy with as few waste products as possible; Use renewable resources from plant sources; Have as few steps as possible to eliminate waste and increase the yield; Use catalysts to save energy.

3   They reduce the activation energy required for reactions; reducing the use of heat which typically comes from fossil fuels.

4   a   Company A = 22/25 × 100 = 88%; Company B = 17.5/19 × 100 = 92%.

b   Company B has a higher percentage yield so is more sustainable.

Life cycle assessments (LCAs)

1   A life cycle assessment is an assessment of the environmental impact of the manufacture and use of different materials and products.

2   Resources used, production, use and disposal.

3   a

Stage of LCA	Plastic bag	Paper bag
Source of raw materials	**From ethene, which is produced during cracking of petrochemicals**	Come from trees
Production	Simple process involving no chemical change	**Consumes water and produces acidic gases and greenhouse gases**
Use	Reusable	**Damaged by water and more difficult to reuse**
End of life	Decompose slowly but produce less **solid waste**	Decompose quickly but generate more **solid waste**

b   Any two from: Paper bags come from a renewable source whereas plastic comes from a finite resource; Plastic bags are reusable but decompose slowly at the end of their life whereas paper bags can't be reused easily but decompose quickly at the end of their life; Paper bags produce more pollution and consume more water.

4   The supermarket has conducted a selective/shortened/abbreviated LCA, ignoring negative points, e.g. slow decomposition/source materials are finite.

Alternative methods of copper extraction

H 1 a

b   It is not pure copper.

H 2   Smelting and electrolysis use a lot of energy; Copper-rich ores are scarce.

H 3 a   Bioleaching using bacteria; Phytomining using plants; Displacement using iron.

b   i   Bioleaching: produces pure copper so needs little further processing; but is slow.

ii   Phytomining: environmentally friendly; but is slow/requires further processing.

iii   Displacement using iron: can use scrap metal; may increase demand for iron.

Making potable water and waste water treatment

1   Water that is safe to drink – harmful chemicals and microbes have been removed.

2   A pure substance is one element or compound; potable water contains other substances like salts and minerals.

3 a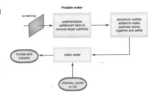

b To sterilise the water.

4 a Reverse osmosis.

b Distillation separates the water from the salt by heating the salt water until the boiling point of water; this requires energy.

5 a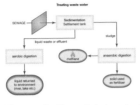

b Removal of harmful chemicals.

Ways of reducing the use of resources

1 a Reduces use of glass bottles; Reduces use of limited raw materials to make other glass products.

b Separation; Reforming; Melting.

2 a It is magnetic.

b Steel is made with iron, carbon and other metals; recycling iron in steel uses the amount of iron needed by extraction from its ore.

c Aluminium extraction uses a lot of energy; which comes from burning fossil fuels – releasing carbon dioxide; recycling aluminium uses less energy.

Rusting

1 Corrosion is the destruction of materials by chemical reactions with substances in the environment.

2 a Test tube 1.

b Rust requires oxygen and water; only test tube 1 is exposed to both oxygen and water; it will rust the most.

c Iron + oxygen + water → hydrated iron(III) oxide

d Test tube 2: No water; Test tube 3: No oxygen; Test tube 4: Paint barrier prevents oxygen or water contacting the iron; Test tube 5: Galvanised with a more reactive metal – stops oxygen or water contacting the iron and, as the metal is more reactive, it will oxidise instead of iron.

e Magnesium or zinc; because it is more reactive; it will react instead of iron.

Alloys as useful materials

1 An alloy is a mixture of metals.

2 a Gold is soft; alloys are harder.

b Gold ions are arranged in layers; Gold ions can slide over each other.

c Copper atoms are a different size to gold atoms; disrupting the layers of gold atoms which makes it more difficult for them to overlap.

---

3 a Car bodywork needs to be hard but still bendable into shape; more carbon makes it strong.

b Sample A, because it contains more carbon so is hardest.

H c M_r iron = 55.8 – number of moles = 24.80/55.8 = 0.4444 moles.
% = 0.444/0.461 × 100 = 96.1%

M_r carbon = 12 – number of moles = 0.21/12 = 0.0175 moles.
% = 0.0175/0.461 × 100 = 3.9%
(ignore rounding errors)

Ceramics, polymers and composites

1 a

Borosilicate glass	High melting point	Silicon dioxide and boron trioxide
Fibre glass	Strong and light	Strands of glass fibre and plastic resin
Ceramics	Hard, brittle, electrical insulators, waterproof	Metal ions and covalent structures

b Ceramic

c Glass fibres reinforce the material; plastic resin is the supporting matrix.

d A composite.

e Fibre glass is light; and strong.

2 a i LDPE
ii HDPE
iii Thermoplastic
iv Thermosetting plastic

b HDPE and LDPE are both produced from chains of the monomer ethene; HDPE has few branches; meaning intermolecular forces are maximised; LDPE has many branches; therefore HDPE is strong and has a higher melting point.

c Milk bottles are made of thermoplastic so can be melted down to make new products; plastic electrical componenets are made of thermosetting plastic so can't be melted down; thermosetting plastics form strong bonds between strands when they set; thermoplastics have weak intermolecular forces between strands.

The Haber process

1 Ammonia

2 $N_2 + 3H_2 \rightarrow 2NH_3$

3 The reaction is reversible and the forward reaction is exothermic. This means that the backward reaction is endothermic.

4 The conditions used are a temperature of 450°C; a pressure of 200–250 atmospheres; and an iron catalyst.

H 5 As the forward reaction is exothermic, it would be favoured by lowering the temperature; the problem is that a low

---

temperature would make the reaction slow; compromise is arrived 450°C; forward reaction reduces number of moles of gas; increasing pressure favours forward reaction; an iron catalyst is used to speed up the reaction.

H 6 a Few molecules of gas in forward reaction; higher pressure favours fewer molecules of gas.

b Higher temperatures reduce percentage yield of ammonia; but lower temperatures make the reaction too slow.

c i 300 atmospheres and 400°C = 50%
ii 200 atmospheres and 350°C = 54% (accept ± 2 percentage points)

Production and uses of NPK fertilisers

1 Plants need compounds of **Nitrogen (N)**, **Phosphorous (P)** and **Potassium (K)** for the growth and carrying out photosynthesis. **Fertilisers** containing these three elements are called **NPK fertilisers**.

2

Ammonium nitrate, NH_4NO_3	Ammonia from the Haber process is oxidised to form nitric acid which is then reacted with ammonia
Ammonium hydrogen phosphate, $(NH_4)_2HPO_4$	Mined phosphate rock is reacted with nitric acid to form phosphoric acid, H_3PO_4, which is reacted with ammonia.
Potassium chloride, KCl	Obtained by mining

3 Different crops/plants have different nutrient needs; their soil may be lacking in particular nutrients

4

Fertiliser	Acid	Alkali
Ammonium nitrate	nitric acid	ammonia
Ammonium phosphate	phosphoric acid	ammonia
Ammonium sulfate	sulfuric acid	ammonia
Potassium nitrate	nitric acid	potassium hydroxide

5 Atomic mass of phosphorous = 31
Molecular mass of ammonium hydrogen phosphate = 132
31/132 x 100 = 23.5%

H 6 Atomic mass of nitrogen (x2) = 28
Molecular mass of ammonium nitrate = 80
28/80 = 35% 0.35x500g = 175 grams
175/28 = 6.25 moles
Or
N_2 and $(NH_4)_2HPO_4$ have 2 atoms of nitrogen; there is a 1:1 ratio; 500/80 = 6.25 moles

For answers to the Practice Papers, visit: www.scholastic.co.uk/gcse